My dear friend and former student, Gloire Emmanual Ndongala, ha ... challenges the weak and seemingly faltering American church to "grow up." His insights are provocative, and his challenge is stinging at times, yet hopeful. I highly recommend this text to all my fellow ministers, church leaders, and any follower of Jesus who longs to push past the 'growing pains' in order to develop the spiritual muscle required for last days spiritual conflict.

Dr. Scott Camp
Evangelist, Author, Educator
www.scottcamp.org

Gloire Ndongala has written a book that will certainly awaken the sleeping church. As a church, we say that we believe the Bible, but we are yet to expect the God of the early Church to do through us what He did through the early disciples and more. Gloire did not just write another book, he has put on paper the fire that burns within him about the Lord and His endless power and love.

Dr. Chantal Yobuoe
Bachelor's in Finance, Masters in French Humanities, master's in ministry, Doctorate in Ministry, Vision International University
Senior Pastor, Rapha Word Church DFW

As a musician, preacher, and personal trainer I believe more than ever that God is on the brink of sending another move of His Spirit as in the days of historical revivals past. In the same breath, I say that this move will not last without a mature church to steward it. I have known my dear friend Gloire for a decade now, and his consistent passion, hunger, and zeal to see a bride that's compatible with Jesus on all levels and is ready for the return of Jesus is far above the status quo. This book will cause you to acknowledge our current lack in the church in the knowledge of God, but I believe it will also stir a hunger after truth and righteousness. We want to be a church made ready and able to maturely steward the presence of God in a greater measure. May this book stir, convict, and encourage you and the generations to come to "grow up" and be all that God intended His church to be.

Cade Leuschner
Musician & Intercessory Missionary, Meleah House of Prayer
Founder of Forerunner Fitness

Reading Grow Up Church is like gaining a glimpse into how the early church functioned. It sheds light on the miraculous deeds of the body of Christ that have been forgotten. For those seeking to return to the simplicity of the body of Christ and discover the complexity of our God, this book is a must. The truths that have been ignored and long since forgotten will be returned to those who seek them. If you are seeking truth, your purpose in this life and how you fit in the body of Christ, this book is for you. I was personally challenged and convicted by this book which brought forth in me new kindling of my faith in Christ and affirmation of who I am in Christ.

1

Melonie Parmley, DO
Disciple of Christ
Doctorate in Osteopathy, Des Moines University

I received an advance copy of Grow Up, Church and said to myself, "Finally, someone who speaks the truth as it was meant to be said!" We live in an era where Scripture is twisted into false radical ideologies. Churches are too afraid to offend, or they twist the Word to fit what they want in their church, rather than what God has called the church to be. Gloire Emmanuel Ndongala dives into the truth of Scripture, as we should, and studies the gifts we have all been given by God. It is a book that will help you discover your gifts and how they can be used effectively based on SCRIPTURE! It is from the wisdom of God, not the knowledge of this world, that Gloire Emmanuel Ndongala can effectively call the church to GROW UP!

Britani Overman
Flight Attendant
Editor at Tamara Taylor Edu Publishing
Bachelor's Degree in English Literature, University of Colorado

I have known Gloire for more than 10 years now. We went to college together, played basketball together, we've prayed together, and we have both seen each other's families grow one kid at a time. We have both seen each other in our lowest points and in our highest points. You really get to see someone's true character at their lowest point. For Gloire, he never changed who he was in Christ when at his lowest point. He never stopped following Christ, when he was completely justified to do so during the toughest battles of his life.
His devotion to God is unmatched, his love for his family is evident, and his loyalty to his friends is like no other. He is a man of the Word, and a man of prayer, and a man passionate for the bride of Christ.
In his book, there is a Jeremiah 6:16 feel, where the Lord said, "Ask for the ancient paths, ask where the good way is, and walk in it, and you will find rest for your souls." Generally speaking, I believe the church has strayed away from the original path God intended. In this book, I believe Gloire, through deep research and prayer, has done a fine job redirecting the church back to the ancient paths. I believe every church and seminary should adopt this book in their libraries, courses, and discipleship programs. God has truly breathed on this book!

Matt Daniels
High School Campus Mentor
Certified Life Coach/Counselor
Worship Minister
Bachelor's Degree in Education

Gloire is undeniably a vessel sent by God for such a time as this. His life of integrity and heart of passion is contiguous. I met Gloire in college with a group of students who were sold out for Jesus. He led prayers meetings where miracles, signs, and wonders happened regularly. His impact on my life is beyond my ability to describe. I have watched Gloire grow over the years and the tools he provides in this book are not just from his mind and heart, but from real experience. This book is very beneficial to anyone called to leadership or even those who desire to mature and develop on a personal level. Gloire does a great job with providing quality information and examining the reading through assessments within the book. Every individual should experience growth when finished reading this book.

Astacia Jones
Behavior Counselor, Newman International Academy
MA in Psychology
www.lifeabandon.com

I've known Gloire for over five years now. We've laughed and cried together. You never really know someone until you've had the opportunity to live under the same roof. In 2015 Gloire and his family moved in with me. As they lived at my house I grew spiritually in many ways. He never sugar coated anything while he stayed with me yet every time, he finished speaking to me, although it was challenging at times, I still knew he cared. His book is an embodiment of his heart for the church.
The church of the end times must grow up. We need to start seeking solid food and stop being kept alive by milk. This book is an amazing book to chew on daily. It is filled with biblical knowledge and spirit-led teachings that all believers need in these days. Enjoy and soak up each word!

Tanya Harper
Owner, Pioneer Bar, TNT Casino, Water to Wine Steakhouse & Terrace
Owner, Jamerica Rentals

I met Gloire during undergrad over 11 years ago. Through my graduate studies, my career as both a pastor and a missionary, and now my layperson's work of bringing my calling to the secular workplace, I can confidently say that he is not only a model example of a fully committed follower of Christ, but also a highly loyal friend. In all the time I've known him, he's been full of integrity, grace, and love for all who come into his path. Gloire is also full of a prophetic fire that I've never seen in anyone else. His passion to see the church of Jesus Christ thrive is unparalleled. I got the immense privilege of reading this book early and can wholly say that it will challenge, push, and grow all who read it. Gloire's writing style is conversational and his words clear. We must grow up as a church, put aside the milk, and sustain ourselves on the meat of the Word. May the truths of this book change you the same way it has changed me.

Jose Lopez
M.A. Theological Studies, Evangel University

B.A. Church Ministries, SAGU

Grow Up, Church
© 2019 Gloire Emmanuel Ndongala

Scripture quotations are from The Holy Bible,
English Standard Version (ESV) unless otherwise stated.

Authors contact details:
Email: gloire041988@gmail.com
Instagram: Gloire777
Facebook: Gloire Emmanuel Ndongala

Published by,
Gloire Emmanuel Ndongala

ISBN: 978-1-7334909-3-1
ISBN: 978-1-7334909-1-7

For the Glory of God

Grow Up, Church

Gloire Emmanuel Ndongala

Acknowledgements

This book could not have been written if it had not been first inspired in me by the Holy Spirit. I believe the Holy Spirit gave me this book to help individuals grow in various areas of their faith.

I would also like to thank Katie, my wife and best friend. She and I have been through unimaginable things, yet by the grace of God, He has shown himself stronger in our weaknesses. When I doubted that God could truly use me to write, Katie would always combat those lies with the truth of what God says about me. She has truly been a rock in my life.

I also would like to thank all of my professors who believed and invested in me. If not for those who taught and poured into me at Southwestern Assemblies of God University, I would have no idea how to truly study the Word of God.

I'd like to thank my mom, as well, who has been another inspiration in my life. She taught me how to pray and sacrificed so much every day so my family could succeed. She was the only one there for my siblings and I, and she did her best to raise us. When she was unable to care for us, she entrusted me in the hands of the Lucero family, who has become a second family to me.

Lastly, I'd like to thank what I like to call "gospel friends." These are friends who have challenged, encouraged, and pushed me into the calling God has for me. It is through their prayers that my life is where it is today!

Table of Contents

Introduction……………………………………………………………………… 9
Chapter 1: Missionary?………………………………………………………… 12
Chapter 2: The Gifts are Dead………………………………………………… 16
Chapter 3: Blaspheming the Holy Spirit……………………………………… 20
Chapter 4: Jimmy, Sadee, and the Church…………………………………… 22
Chapter 5: Jimmy and the Church……………………………………………… 25
Chapter 6: Monopoly Money…………………………………………………… 32
Chapter 7: Sadee and the School……………………………………………… 34
Chapter 8: Immaturity…………………………………………………………… 38
Chapter 9: The Church System………………………………………………… 44
Chapter 10: Worship or Praise………………………………………………… 55
Chapter 11: Maturing in How We Decipher God's Word…………………… 62
Chapter 12: The Complex Us…………………………………………………… 73
Chapter 13: The Personality Gifts: My Spirit………………………………… 79
Chapter 14: Service……………………………………………………………… 84
Chapter 15: The One Who Teaches…………………………………………… 88
Chapter 16: The One Who Exhorts…………………………………………… 91
Chapter 17: In His Generosity………………………………………………… 95
Chapter 18: The One Who Leads……………………………………………… 98
Chapter 19: One Who Does Acts of Mercy………………………………… 103
Chapter 20: The Gift of Hospitality…………………………………………… 107
Chapter 21: The Gifts of Operation: My Soul……………………………… 110
Chapter 22: The Oral Gifts…………………………………………………… 117
Chapter 23: Interpretations of Tongues…………………………………… 121
Chapter 24: Prophecy………………………………………………………… 127
Chapter 25: The Knowing Gifts: Word of Knowledge……………………… 133
Chapter 26: The Knowing Gifts: Word of Wisdom………………………… 139
Chapter 27: The Knowing Gifts: Discernment of Spirits…………………… 143
Chapter 28: Deliverance and the Gift of Discernment……………………… 152
Chapter 29: The Knowing Gifts and Dream Interpretation………………… 157
Chapter 30: The Power Gifts: Faith………………………………………… 163
Chapter 31: The Gift of Healing……………………………………………… 173
Chapter 32: Healing and Deliverance……………………………………… 177
Chapter 33: The Working of Miracles……………………………………… 188
Chapter 34: The Parental Gifts: My Body………………………………… 194
Chapter 35: The Hand Models the Parenting Gifts………………………… 200
Chapter 36: The Apostle……………………………………………………… 204
Chapter 37: The Prophet……………………………………………………… 212
Chapter 38: The Evangelist…………………………………………………… 224
Chapter 39: The Pastor……………………………………………………… 232
Chapter 40: The Teacher……………………………………………………… 242
Chapter 41: Conclusion……………………………………………………… 249
Tests…………………………………………………………………………… 254
Notes…………………………………………………………………………… 268

INTRODUCTION

When you look in the book of Acts at the way the early church operated and compare it to how our churches operate today, it's obvious that we're far from the original model. Some may argue that it's because cultures change over time, and they would say that it's necessary to change the way the church operates. While this is true, the Word of God should never change.

I'm going to biblically try to tackle what I see as the biggest issue plaguing the church, which is immaturity. **For the purpose of this book, I'm defining immaturity as an individual's inability to take Biblical truth and allow it to permeate their heart.** This results in an inability to bear the fruit of godliness in their day-to-day interactions with people.

I'm also going to look at how we can maturely implement biblical truths in the modern-day church structure. God's house cannot be filled with disorder, and through this book, my goal is to explain how to establish God's intended order in the church and how it functions.

Paul addressed the issues of confusion, disorder, and immaturity in the early church as well. The church in Corinth was a church that was flowing in the gifts of the Spirit yet was immature in how believers interacted with each other and in the orderly use of the gifts. This led Paul to make the statement, "For God is not a God of disorder but of peace--as in all the congregations of the Lord's people" (*1 Corinthians 14.33, NIV*).

How do you combat disorder, confusion, and immaturity in the church? The answer is simple: we must look at what God's Word says and apply it. The early church understood that God's leadership structure allowed people to grow and mature.

There are always going to be immature people in the church because we are all in different levels with the Lord. There is, however, a difference between progressive maturity and stagnant immaturity. First John says this,

"I am writing to you, little children,

because your sins are forgiven for his name's sake.

I am writing to you, fathers,

because you know him who is from the beginning.

I am writing to you, young men,

because you have overcome the evil one.

I write to you, children,

because you know the Father.

I write to you, fathers,

because you know him who is from the beginning.

I write to you, young men,

because you are strong,

and the word of God abides in you,

and you have overcome the evil one." (1 John 2:12-14)

Clearly, when one looks at this passage, one can see that there are children in the church. By children, John is not speaking about merely a child, but a new believer. Keeping in step with this thought process, John talks about fathers and young men.

With this in mind, the premise of my book is in no way coming against new believers. On the contrary, it's about not condoning behaviors of Christians who have been saved for years and still drink milk instead of eating solid foods as an adult should, as God would expect them to in season.

My hope is that, by the end of this book, you will understand how to grow into spiritual maturity and will be ready to move forward in the fullness of who God has called you to be.

CHAPTER 1

Missionary?

It was 2004 and I'd been invited to church by a girl I had a crush on. I was 16 years old at the time and overly confident in myself because of my athletic ability. I walked into the church, found a seat in the back, and sat there in quiet anticipation.

What was I anticipating? Well, this was not my first time at a church. I'd attended plenty of Congolese churches prior to this, because I was born in the Congo and it was expected of me to attend. But in every Congolese church I went to, something crazy always happened. People would sometimes break out in dance, and other times, they'd literally be foaming at the mouth. With those experiences in my mind, I was anticipating something crazy here.

Service started and progressed in a low-key, normal way, however. No crazy manifestations, no jubilant dancing, and definitely no foaming at the mouth. Afterwards, the pastor asked me if I wanted to go to camp with the youth group and he said they would pay for me. I was hesitant until he said, "we will be playing basketball." *Basketball?* They could count me in!

We lived in Colorado, and the church had a place in the beautiful Rockies where they camped. I remember driving up in the bus and getting my first glimpse of the campsite. It was very remote; there wasn't a house within thirty blocks. All I saw were dorms and a basketball hoop outside.

We unloaded our bags and went to our dorms. We had to get ready quickly since it was dinner time. When we finished eating, we played a little game of basketball before service started. When we all went inside, the lights were off and there were some green lights on the stage. There was a full band and they started to sing. As soon as they did, I started to feel something I had never felt before, like water mixed with fire all over my body.

This presence, full of love, hit me like a semi-truck. As I was consumed in this presence, it was like my whole life flashed before my eyes. My dream had always been to go to the NBA, but somehow, in this moment, I knew that anything that I could ever hope to accomplish would pale in comparison to the greatness of God.

I surrendered my life to God in that moment, and that was the beginning of me discovering who God created me to be. That moment opened the door to such a passion, I could hardly hold myself together. Prior to this encounter, it seemed like every time I attended a service, someone who was speaking would stop and look at me while they were speaking and say, "You're going to be a great man of God, and God has called you to the nations."

I never understood what that meant. *Nations? How do I go? When do I go? How do I prepare for this?* I never really knew what to do with the things people would tell me, so I just wondered about them. In this moment, though, in the presence of God, these questions began to race through my mind.

Sometimes at church, missionaries would come and share about the places they'd been. As I would listen to them, I always felt like my heart would burst out of my chest as they'd speak. Somehow, deep down inside, I knew I was supposed to be a missionary.

In John 7:3-5, Jesus' brother challenges Him by indirectly questioning if He truly is the Messiah. Verse 5 says, "For not even his brothers believed in him." This passage always astonished me. Jesus' brothers lived in the same house, and according to eastern traditions, probably slept in the same room for 20 plus years. Yet, they did not believe in Him.

This lets us know that a person can be living with Jesus, and Jesus can still not be living in them. This was my life. I grew up in a Christian home, but Christ did not live in me until this moment at camp.

My youth pastor, Joel Sosa, had attended a school in Texas called Southwestern Assemblies of God University (SAGU). When he took us to visit the school during my junior year of high school, I knew this was where I was going to go in order to become a missionary.

While at SAGU, I grew beyond belief. I learned so much about the Bible and it's also where I found my wife (can I get an amen?). But I still remember the class that helped shape my mentality today. One of my professors, who was the professor of Intercultural Studies, made a statement to our class that was life-altering for me. "The word missionary is not found in the Bible, it's really the word 'apostle,'" he said.

Wait what?

"The word 'apostle' in the Greek is 'Apostolos', which means 'sent forth'," he explained. I remember looking around the class, but no one else seemed to be as affected by his statement as I was. Since I got saved, all I dreamed of was being a missionary, and now my dream was crushed.

I thought, *if it's not in the Bible and the real name is apostle, why do we call people missionaries?* This was the beginning of a journey that lead to me discovering the fivefold ministry.

So, I started studying the fivefold ministry. As I did, I began realizing how important it is to the Body of Christ. If the church could be compared to a basketball team, the fivefold ministry would be the dream team. There is a total of five different offices: apostle, prophet, evangelist, pastor, and teacher. When each of these offices operate together, they help the church body grow and mature.

CHAPTER 2

The Gifts are Dead

Before we move into more deeply examining the fivefold ministry and the function of each office in the body of Christ, we must first get a good biblical understanding of the gifts. To comprehend the importance of the gifts we must first look at Numbers 11. Moses has just brought the children of Israel out of bondage through the power of God, and they are now in the desert. Instead of being joyful and content, however, the people began to grumble against Moses and God.

Although most of them were adults, all but a handful of them were spiritually immature. This is clearly evidenced by their grumbling, which is what babies and small children do when they don't get their way. Moses eventually became fed up and pleaded with God about the situation.

"Moses said to the Lord, 'Why have you dealt ill with your servant? And why have I not found favor in your sight, that you lay the burden of all this people on me? Did I conceive all this people? Did I give them birth, that you should say to me, 'Carry them in your bosom, as a nurse carries a nursing child,' to the land that you swore to give their fathers? Where am I to get meat to give to all this people? For they weep before me and say, 'Give us meat, that we may eat.' I am not able to carry all this people alone; the burden is too heavy for me. If you will treat me like this, kill me at once, if I find favor in your sight, that I may not see my wretchedness.'"
(Numbers 11: 10-15)

Moses could see his demise. He realized that one man could not carry the burden of a whole group of people. He was experiencing burnout. But God knows what we need and when we're overwhelmed, He already has the solution ready for us.

"Then the Lord said to Moses, 'Gather for me seventy men of the elders of Israel, whom you know to be the elders of the people and officers over them, and bring them to the tent of meeting, and let them take their stand there with you. And I will come down and talk with you there. And I will take some of the Spirit that is on you and put it on them, and they shall bear the burden of the people with you, so that you may not bear it yourself alone.'" (Numbers 11: 16-17)

The solution wasn't that Moses needed more of God, but that Moses needed others to help him accomplish the will of God. **The goal isn't to become a one-man show. The goal is to be unified as one.** Coming together as one body helps reveal the gospel to the world. Jesus' prayer echoes this in John 17:2:

"I do not ask for these only, but also for those who will believe in me through their word, that they may all be one, just as you, Father, are in me, and I in you, that they also may be in us, so that the world may believe that you have sent me. The glory that you have given me I have given to them, that they may be one even as we are one, I in them and you in me, that they may become perfectly one, so that the world may know that you sent me and loved them even as you loved me."

God took the Spirit that was upon Moses and shared it with the other elders, and all but two of them prophesied once and stopped. Two of the elders continued to prophesy amongst the people. Joshua, who would later lead the children of Israel into the Promised Land, learned of this. And how did he react to them prophesying?

"And a young man ran and told Moses, 'Eldad and Medad are prophesying in the camp.' And Joshua the son of Nun, the assistant of Moses from his youth, said, 'My lord Moses, stop them.'" (v. 27-28)

Stop them? Why would Joshua want to stop them? **You see, I believe they had grown so accustomed to Moses running the show that they started to look at Moses as though he was God.** They seemed to feel that only Moses could operate in the gifts so freely.

But what was Moses' response?

"But Moses said to him, 'Are you jealous for my sake? Would that all the Lord's people were prophets, that the Lord would put his Spirit on them!'" (v. 29)

This verse reveals the heart God. He is not exclusive, but inclusive. This is echoed in Joel 2:28-29:

"And it shall come to pass afterward, that I will pour out my Spirit on all flesh; your sons and your daughters shall prophesy, your old men shall dream dreams, and your young men shall see visions. Even on the male and female servants in those days I will pour out my Spirit."

It's clear that Moses longed for a day when everyone would be able to operate as a mouthpiece for God. Why, then, would we regress? *If the Old Testament is the gospel concealed and the New Testament is the gospel revealed, why would we want the gifts to remain sealed?*

Jesus declares to his disciples,

"Truly, truly, I say to you, whoever believes in me will also do the work that I do; and greater works than these will he do, because I am going to the Father. Whatever you ask in my name, this I will do, that the Father may be glorified in the Son. If you ask me anything in my name, I will do it." (John 14:12-14)

According to Jesus, we are supposed to do more now, not less. We are supposed to operate Just like He did. He only did what He saw His Father doing. Shouldn't we do the same?

CHAPTER 3

Blaspheming the Holy Spirit

Right before Jesus was crucified, He spoke to His disciples about the Holy Spirit. He made sure they understood the importance of the Spirit of God falling on them and being in them. He even said that it was better for Him to leave, because if He didn't, the Holy Spirit wouldn't come (John 16:7).

The significance of the Spirit of God in our lives cannot truly be explained in its entirety, no matter how many books we read, movies we watch, or teachings we study. Truly, to get even a little understanding of our need for Him in our lives, we must resign our life to Him and give Him full control.

How precious is the Holy Spirit? Jesus once said to the Pharisees that blaspheming the Holy Spirit was an unforgivable sin. And what exactly is blaspheming the Holy Spirit?

In Matthew 12, Jesus is healing people on the Sabbath and the religious crowd, namely the Pharisees, are jealous and bitter toward Him because people are starting to follow Him instead of them. So, they accuse Jesus of using demons to cast out demons. Jesus then explains to them that a house divided cannot stand, and that even Satan's kingdom is not divided. In verse 27 Jesus says,

"And if I cast out demons by Beelzebul, by whom do your sons cast them out? Therefore, they will be your judges. But if it is by the Spirit of God that I cast out demons, then the kingdom of God has come upon you...Therefore I tell you,

every sin and blasphemy will be forgiven people, but the blasphemy against the Spirit will not be forgiven. And whoever speaks a word against the Son of Man will be forgiven, but whoever speaks against the Holy Spirit will not be forgiven, either in this age or in the age to come" (vv. 27-31).

What was it that the Pharisees did that caused Jesus to say, "but the blasphemy against the Spirit will not be forgiven"? If we examine this passage more deeply, we get insight into this. They said that Jesus was casting out demons by Beelzebub, which is another name for Baal or Satan. But was their statement what really caused them to be rebuked so harshly, or the heart behind it?

I firmly believe that the Pharisees were blaspheming or in danger of blaspheming the Holy Spirit **because they consciously attributed what the Holy Spirit was doing to the devil.** But if Jesus said it was through the power of the Holy Spirit that He cast out devils, and He rebuked the Pharisees for saying that it was actually Satan working in Him, why are we so quick to say that those who operate in the gifts are being used of the devil? Why do some say that people who speak in tongues are speaking in a satanic language? Have we no fear?

For a person to see someone who is operating in the gifts of the Spirit and then to say, "they are possessed by a demon," or to even entertain that thought process, is provoking judgment.

CHAPTER 4

Jimmy, Sadee, and the Church

This next story I'm going to share is based on a true story. To protect those involved, certain names and events have been changed, but the core of the message is the same.

Jimmy and his twin sister had always been close, but not just because they were twins. Their hearts for God gave them a special bond. Jimmy was a *feeler*, although he would never admit it because he didn't want to feel so feminine. Sadee, on the other hand, was a *thinker*. Both of them felt at a young age that God was calling them to reach the nations with the gospel.

The passage that best described Jimmy was when Paul said, "Do not be slothful in zeal, be fervent in spirit, serve the Lord" (Romans 12:11-12). Zeal, by definition, means *passion, fervor, ardor, or enthusiasm*. It also means *intense emotion and compelling action.*[1] Passion applies to an emotion that is deeply stirring or ungovernable. Furthermore, the word *fervent* reflects the word *zeal*. **Biblically speaking, someone who is a feeler is someone who leans toward being zealous.**

On the other hand, someone who is a thinker, like Sadee, would be accurately depicted by Proverbs 19:2: "Even zeal is no good without knowledge, and he who hurries his footsteps misses the mark." (BSB) The word for "knowledge" in Hebrew is *dah'-ath,* and it has many different meanings depending on where and how it is used in the Bible. Strong's Exhaustive Concordance describes this word as "cunning, ignorantly, knowledge, unawares wittingly." **Thinkers are people who lean more on their knowledge, and this is how they process the world.**

Jimmy and Sadee grew up in the small town of Bismarck, North Dakota. They had always wanted to go to different places and share the gospel. After graduating high school, Jimmy *felt* and Sadee *thought* that God wanted them to go to a Christian university. Jimmy prayed until he felt God say that he should go to Alabama Christ-Centered University. But Sadee also prayed and she couldn't really hear what God was saying, so she used her wisdom and found out which Christian universities could give her the best scholarships. It just happened to be Alabama Christ-Centered University. So that's where she decided to go.

When they got to the university, both of them felt God lead them to different degree programs. Jimmy ended up graduating with a bachelor's degree in Church Leadership. Sadee, on the other hand, earned a Bachelor's in Psychology. After they both graduated, they began to pray about where God would want to use them. They preferred to stay in their current denomination because this was the main denomination of the university.

These two twins were inseparable, and they wanted to do life together if they could. So, one day when Jimmy told Sadee that he felt God was calling him to go to Maine, she couldn't help but desire to go too. She quickly looked for a Christian school where she could get her master's degree in Social Work. She researched and found The College of Theophilus in Rockport, Maine. They apparently had an amazing social work program, so she sent in her application. Within two weeks, she was accepted.

She shared the news with Jimmy. This was a confirmation for him, so he said, "let's just pack our car and go, and God will provide." Sadee, on the other hand, thought it would be much wiser to make sure that they had a place to stay first. She searched online and found a house for rent not too far from the school. She contacted the owner and discovered that house was a two-story home, with the spacious second floor housing two bedrooms.

She told Jimmy about it, and he responded with yet another confirmation and began to thank God. Sadee was excited too, but she was so shy that it was hard to tell when she was excited. Jimmy could tell his sister was excited though, because they were so close.

They packed their car and headed off to Rockport. Jimmy believed that God wanted him to share the gospel with the people of Rockport, but he didn't quite know what this would look like. As usual, he just trusted God.

They arrived about two weeks before Sadee started school. During these two weeks, Jimmy searched for a church for them. He looked online and found a church called Our Freedom in Christ Assembly (OFCA). One Sunday morning, Jimmy and Sadee decided to visit the church.

When they walked in, there weren't too many people and it was a much older crowd. Second guessing their decision, they hesitantly took their seats.

CHAPTER 5

Jimmy and the Church

After the service was over, the youth pastor greeted Jimmy and Sadee. Noticing the boots and flannel shirts that Sadee and Jimmy wore, he asked, "What are you guys doing out in this part of town?"

"Well, I felt like God was calling us out here, so we came," Jimmy responded.

"You guys wanna go to the park after service? We can stop by somewhere and get a bite to eat. On me," the youth pastor said.

Jimmy and Sadee, accustomed to being hungry college students, said, "Count us in!"

While at the park, Jimmy and Sadee learned that the youth pastor was actually the senior pastor's son. "What would you like to do here at the church? How would you like to serve?" the youth pastor asked.

"I'll do whatever God wants me to do," Jimmy replied.

"Well what do you think about being the children's pastor at our church? We'll need to run a background check first, though, and we wouldn't be able to pay you right away."

"Let me pray about it and get back to you," said Jimmy.

After praying for a week, Jimmy and Sadee both felt like this is what they were supposed to do. So, they notified the youth pastor, who then got the idea approved by his father. Now, the youth pastor's father and mother were older and had considered retiring. So, the youth pastor said to Jimmy, "My father and mother are going to step down here very soon. Once they do, we will be able to pay you a better salary. For the time being though, the church has agreed to help as much as they can."

Jimmy jumped right in and started participating at the church. However, he felt like something was off. He noticed that people in the church would avoid speaking to the youth pastor face to face for whatever reason. He brought this up to the youth pastor, who brushed it off like it was no big deal.

Jimmy continued working faithfully with the children. By the grace of God, Jimmy's ministry started to grow. He did small outreaches and prayed that God would bring in people to the church. God answered his prayers, and the small children's ministry continued to grow.

Now Jimmy also started helping with the youth because the youth pastor wanted him to be part of the leadership. At the time, the leadership consisted of the youth pastor's father (the lead pastor and lead elder), his wife (the Sunday school teacher), and the youth pastor's wife (the secretary). The youth pastor was also an elder on the board, along with one other elder who oversaw the finances.

One day during praise and worship, Jimmy laid himself prostrate. He often did this to honor God. Suddenly, something slammed against his ribcage, knocking the wind out of him. Surprised and out of breath, he looked up and saw the youth pastor standing over him saying. "Get up," the youth pastor said.

Shocked and in pain, Jimmy sat up and dragged himself to the nearest pew for support. *What just happened?* he thought. He stayed quiet for the rest of the service, gripping his throbbing side.

What would usually happen after service is that Jimmy and Sadee would go over the youth pastor's house for some late-night dinner. Since Sadee was busy with homework, Jimmy drove over to the house by himself, still confused about the incident.

They sat down to eat. Suddenly, the youth pastor's wife spoke. "Why did you hit him?" she asked her husband.

Without skipping a beat, he replied, "I did not hit him."

Shocked, Jimmy jumped in "You did hit me!" he said.

For the next hour, Jimmy and the youth pastor's wife continued to press the issue with the youth pastor until he finally said, "Yes I did hit you, I'm sorry."

When Jimmy went home, he shared the details of the evening with Sadee, hoping to get more understanding. "There are probably more things happening than this," she said.

Now, Jimmy knew that he couldn't leave the church unless God directed him to do so, so he stayed. One day while he was at the youth pastor's house, the youth pastor's wife persuaded the youth pastor to share what had been happening in their marriage. Reluctantly, he shared how they were both abusing each other.

His wife quickly chimed in. "Both?" she said. "Why don't you tell him about all the different things you did to me, like hitting me so hard that I went through a wall."

Jimmy left their house, shocked and overwhelmed. He tried to call one of his college professors for counsel, but the professor was busy and unable to talk. Jimmy spoke to Sadee about the situation, and she gave Jimmy some wise advice. "You need to speak to the wife and find out what she wants to do," she said.

Jimmy contacted the youth pastor's wife, making sure her husband was there to hear as well. "What would you like to do in this situation?" Jimmy asked.

"I want restoration," she responded. "Can you and Sadee help us?"

Her response shocked him, and he and Sadee both concluded that the youth pastors needed professional counseling. So, Jimmy contacted them and shared this with them. But the youth pastor and his wife disagreed. "We've already tried counseling, and it didn't work. This is our last resort."

Jimmy and Sadee then decided to try and do some pastoral counseling with them. When they all showed up for the first meeting, Sadee shared with them that restoration had to be something they each would agree to work toward. They agreed to try.

The first meeting, however, ended up being a disaster. For six hours, the youth pastor refused to admit to be an abuser. After leaving the meeting, Sadee, being wise, spoke to Jimmy and said, "This will not work. It will drain the life out of you." But Jimmy, who thought his gift of faith could solve anything, didn't listen.

Jimmy tried to help them out by doing some more pastoral counseling. The youth pastor, however, was still stubborn. Hoping to change the situation, Jimmy advised them to tell the senior pastor. They decided not to, as the senior pastor was elderly, and they thought it would break his heart and possibly kill him.

But Jimmy knew they needed accountability, so he suggested having the financial board member present. *This will settle the situation,* Jimmy thought. But what Jimmy didn't know is that the board member had become loyal to the family and viewed the youth pastor's wife as a troublemaker.

So instead of getting help from him, Jimmy now had to speak to that board member about his role as an elder and the accountability that came with it. Although this board member was way older than Jimmy by at least 30 years, it seemed that he had only grown physically but was still spiritually immature.

The conclusion that Jimmy, the youth pastor, and the board member reached was that once a week, they would all meet and hold the youth pastor accountable. They would ask him how his marriage was going and challenge him to make changes to help his family get healthier.

As these weekly meetings started, however, it became obvious that the youth pastor didn't want to submit. He would always have a way of twisting the conversation so that Jimmy was seen as the troublemaker. At one meeting, the youth pastor, in tears, spoke up and said, "I feel as though Jimmy is judging me."

Jimmy responded by saying "1 Corinthians 5 says we are supposed to judge those who are in church. This does not mean condemn them, but it does mean to not condone their sin." The board member, hoping to be the peacekeeper, responded by defending the youth pastor.

Jimmy continued to push the memo though, because knew that **true love cannot be devoid of truth.** So, he read the requirements of an elder to them from Titus 1:6-9:

"If anyone is above reproach, the husband of one wife, and his children are believers and not open to the charge of debauchery or insubordination. For an overseer, as God's steward, must be above reproach. He must not be arrogant or

*quick-tempered or a drunkard or violent or greedy for gain, but hospitable, a lover of good, self-controlled, upright, holy, and disciplined. He must hold firm to the trustworthy word as taught, so that he may be able to give instruction in sound doctrine and **also to rebuke those who contradict it."***

Jimmy could not understand why these seasoned Christians couldn't come to terms with what the Bible was saying. **It seemed that the Word of God had penetrated their minds but had yet to truly permeate in their hearts.**

Things got so bad in their marriage that Jimmy spoke to the board member and youth pastor about how the youth pastor needed to step down for a time to get his house in order. The plan was that someone would fill in for him as they took the time to get some more professional counseling.

Although the youth pastor agreed, he still managed to control things in the youth ministry. Jimmy ended up filling in for the youth pastor during this time of "restoration." The senior pastor, however, started becoming aggravated by the situation. In his eyes, this was a hostile takeover. Because he was oblivious to the youth pastor's marriage issue, he thought Jimmy was trying to take over the church.

The youth pastor slowly used his relationship with his father as a way to get back into his original position. **Jimmy, who had faith but lacked wisdom to know when to move on, started feeling overwhelmed and had a nervous breakdown.**

Eventually, many of the youth scattered. The congregation also lost some of its members. Some went into cults while others just stayed at home and vowed to never attend church again. They felt let down by God, when in actuality it was man's system of leadership and his behavior that pulled them out of communion with God.

CHAPTER 6

Monopoly Money

During this time, things were not easy at home for Sadee. You see, Sadee had always been practical. She had grown up using the wisdom God had given her to navigate through life. For her, if she could "see the North Star" (know where the next step was), she would never get lost.

But sometimes it's so foggy or stormy that she couldn't see the North Star. During these times, she would feel helpless. She and Jimmy were struggling financially, but there was nothing she could do. With a full load of classes plus an internship, Sadee had to rely on what Jimmy brought home financially.

She calculated what they would need to earn every month to survive. Rent was $750/month, and Jimmy was only getting paid $250/week, $200 dollars of which was just reimbursement. They still had to eat and pay for gas.

Sadee would often suggest to Jimmy the idea of her getting a job, to which Jimmy would reply, "I feel like we need to walk by faith right now." This would trouble Sadee. For her, trusting God to provide was something she wasn't accustomed to.

Somehow, God would provide every single month. Sometimes people would drop food off at their home, and sometimes people would randomly write them checks. As she witnessed this miraculous provision, she would still try to logically comprehend how all the bills were paid each month.

One day Jimmy and Sadee were talking to their friends on the phone and sharing all the craziness they had experienced so far in life. Their friends were on the other line in utter disbelief. "How do you guys live?" their friends asked. Jimmy jokingly responded, "We live off Monopoly money." Sadee got a kick out of this. It was the perfect analogy; Monopoly money has no real value and they both could relate to this because their finances had no value.

God was using this time in Jimmy and Sadee's lives to help mature them. Although Sadee continued to struggle in her wisdom she knew that God was helping her mature by letting her and Jimmy survive on "Monopoly money."

CHAPTER 7

Sadee and the School

While Jimmy was dealing with the youth pastor, Sadee also had her hands full at school. **At first glance, it seemed like the school was living up to its name, as Theophilus means "lover of God."** However, when she started attending classes, she was met with resistance from every angle.

First, there were the professors. As she was going through her social work program, it seemed as though almost every professor who professed to be a Christian was bent on undermining Christianity. From the get-go, in almost every class Sadee went to, the professors would elevate humanism over godliness.

Sadee refused to compromise her faith and stood strong on the Word of God. This made some of her professors so furious that they graded her papers based on her values instead of the assignment's criteria.

Sadee went to the chairman of the social work department in hopes that he would hear her case and help her out. She told him about the injustice that had been taking place and asked for his help. "The professor who grades your papers has gone through terrible situations in his life," he said. "What you wrote may have touched some wounds he had."

This response seemed very cowardly to Sadee. *Does that give him the right to grade my paper down because he may be offended by it?* she thought. Sadee left frustrated and at a loss for words.

Sadee had a classmate named Becky who lived across the street and would come over from time to time. Becky professed to be a lesbian and was not quiet about it. Sadee and Jimmy loved her and took the time to build a friendship with her.

They would invite her over and cook for her and just hang out with her. Here and there, the topic of gender identity would rise up, and Becky would admit her lifestyle and discuss it with Jimmy and Sadee. They would listen to her but wouldn't budge on what God's Word revealed about homosexuality.

One day, Jimmy was speaking to her and said, "You know, sometimes people who are dealing with gender identity issues were abused when they were younger." Immediately, Becky started crying and admitted that her hatred of men stemmed from being violated at a young age. Jimmy and Sadee continued to talk with her, counseling her and leading her into the truth.

After this conversation, Becky felt free for the first time. She started reading the Bible for herself and truly understood how God saw homosexuality. She realized that it was a sin. She genuinely felt convicted by the Holy Spirit and she knew she could not continue living in that lifestyle. The goal of Sadee and Jimmy's ministry to her was not so that she would fall in love with a man. The goal was to help her to fall in love with Jesus.

Unfortunately, trouble was waiting for her right around the corner. You see, one of Sadee and Becky's professors had grown fond of Becky. This professor had a doctoral degree in psychology, and he was also a pastor. His wife was bedridden due to sickness, so he would usually hire a student to watch their children since she was too sick to care for them. Eventually, he hired Becky.

Viewing him as an honest man, she agreed to work for him. After some time, he invited her to his church. She started becoming more active, attending services and helping with community outreaches.

He began to explain to Becky how he and his wife were just basically roommates. He told her that he did not love her anymore. That the only reason they were still together was for the kids. He continued to tell her that he fell in love with Becky.

Now Sadee and this professor did not get along. She would always hear him say strange things in class and would challenge him on it. He once stated how in some instances, people who have been divorced and remarried would still go and spend time with their old spouses and even sleep in the same bed. This was no big deal to him, but Sadee felt as if he was sharing it because he was up to something devious.

Becky slowly became attached to this professor. She ended up going on a mission trip with the church and while they were there, he deceived her into believing that he loved her and ended up having an affair with her.

When she got back home from her trip, Jimmy came to talk to her about how it went. In his heart, a quiet voice spoke to him and said, "Ask her what happened between her and the professor." So, Jimmy, knowing that it was God speaking asked Becky about it.

She burst into tears. "He loves me, he really loves me," she said.

"If he loved you, he would not have done this to you," Jimmy said. Sadee began comforting Becky and encouraging her to tell the school, but Becky was scared. The professor's wife, who had found out about the incident, condemned Becky for her own husband's actions and tried to lure Becky to their house. It was apparent that she, too, had something up her sleeve.

Sadee wisely encouraged Becky not to go over to their house. Becky felt torn inside because this professor, who had also been her pastor, had used his power and took advantage of her. But Jimmy and Sadee kept telling Becky, "This is not the first time he has done this. Don't fall for his lies." Sure enough, their statement was confirmed. Becky did end up in contact with the professor's wife, who pleaded with her not to notify the school.

"This is not the first time he has done this," she said. "But please don't tell. He will lose his job and if he loses his job, I'm so sick that I can't work so we will lose everything."

Eventually though, Becky did notify the school and they removed him. It was clear to Sadee that the school did not want their image ruined, so they didn't handle the issue as they should have. It was almost swept under the rug.

Where is this pastor now? Well, serving in another church of course. How many victims did this man have? How many lives did he destroy? How come a university that professes to know God can compromise so much? What would have happened if the chairman had taken seriously the biblical compromises of the professors?

This situation left Becky hurt, lost, and confused, and her view of God became distorted. **She went on to spend time in counseling in hopes of regaining a right perspective of God.**

CHAPTER 8

Immaturity

There are many Beckys in the world, hiding in the shadows and silenced by abuse. **If we as a church do not proactively change our ways of handling situations and make sure, to the best of our ability, that things like this don't occur, we could lose a generation due to mistrust.**

I believe immaturity is a large part of the problem. In the introduction, I defined what I believe immaturity to be: an individual's inability to take the Word of God and allow it to permeate his heart.

On October 2, 2016, my wife gave birth to our son, Dóxa. This experience was by far the craziest thing I've ever been through. She was in labor for over 30 hours and I could do nothing to really help ease her pain. I've never felt so helpless in my life! But as the Scripture says,

"When a woman is giving birth, she has sorrow because her hour has come, but when she has delivered the baby, she no longer remembers the anguish, for joy that a human being has been born into the world (John 16:21)."

Truly, my wife felt this way.

The process is no different when it comes to spiritual birth. In John 3, Jesus explains to one of the Pharisees, Nicodemus, that the only way for a human being to be saved is for him to be born again (John 3:3). This shocked Nicodemus because he had never heard of this concept. Yet this is truly the only way to see or enter the Kingdom of God.

When we are sharing Christ with people and helping them come to the light, the process can be frustrating, and in some cases even dangerous. But what joy when we actually see them choose to be born again!

Throughout Scripture, we are compared to children, and just like children we must mature. But how do we mature? I believe God has given us the tools necessary for this process to take place, but it's up to us to use them. Before we explore these tools let's get a better understanding of what immaturity looks like in the church.

Their Fruit Does Not Mature

In Luke 8:5-15, Jesus speaks to the disciples about the parable of the sower. To the crowd he speaks it in a parable, but to his disciples he makes it plain. What I have done in this next paragraph is put both the parable and the response together so you simultaneously can see them and how they correlate. I'm going to focus on one key part of the passage, verses 7 and 14.

Jesus is making an analogy between a seed and the Word of God. He explains that there are four different types of soil (ground) that the seed can be thrown into. Each ground responds to the seed according to its characteristics. Jesus is using this illustration to explain salvation and what hinders the seed (God's Word) from penetrating someone's heart.

"'A sower went out to sow his seed (11 Now the parable is this: The seed is the word of God.). And as he sowed, some fell along the path and was trampled underfoot, and the birds of the air devoured it (12 The ones along the path are those who have heard; then the devil comes and takes away the word from their hearts, so that they may not believe and be saved.) And some fell on the rock, and as it grew up, it withered away, because it had no moisture (13 And the ones on the rock are those who, when they hear the word, receive it with joy. But these have no root; they believe for a while, and in time of testing fall away.) And some fell among thorns, and the thorns grew up with it and choked it (14 And as for what fell among the thorns, they are those who hear, but as they go on their way they are choked by the cares and riches and pleasures of life, and their fruit does not mature.) 8 And some fell into good soil and grew and yielded a hundredfold.' As he said these things, he called out, "He who has ears to hear, let him hear." (15 As for that in the good soil, they are those who, hearing the word, hold it fast in an honest and good heart, and bear fruit with patience)."

Out of the four places the seed is thrown, only one soil "responds" correctly: the good soil. The other three soils are hindered by different things. This means only ¼, or 25%, of people respond well to the Word of God. No wonder God wants us to work together!

The soil symbolizes a person's heart. If we understand this parable, we can better comprehend how to reach people and what is hindering them from responding to the gospel and maturing in it.

The Seed Thrown on the Path

The first one Jesus says the seed is thrown on the path but the birds, who He explains represents Satan, steal it before it has a chance to go in. **I find this rather interesting because I would think if you're on the path, you're safe and you know where you're going.** Apparently, though, it's not about what you can see but about what's beneath.

The Seed Thrown on the Rocks

The next set of seeds fall in the rocks and grows. The people with this type of seed even respond with joy, but just like plants that grow on the mountain side don't have enough soil to dig deep and be grounded, so it is with these types of people. The Bible says they believe for a while. How long is a while? Five, 20, 60 years?

There are some people who will go to church their whole lives, and at the end of the day, they will fit this category. These people will never truly be rooted in the faith, but they'll still look like a tree that's planted.

The Seed Thrown on the Thorns

The third soil is characterized by the cares and riches and pleasures of life. This one to me is the most deceiving one because these people have fruit, but their fruit never reaches maturity. As believers, we are taught that we can know false teachers by their fruit (Matthew 7:15-20). These people have fruit, but it's immature. They believe they are saved, and they even have a level of love, joy, peace, patience, kindness, goodness, faithfulness, gentleness, and self-control (Galatians 5:22-23).

The Seed Thrown on the Good Soil

Only one place the seed was thrown dug deep into the heart, and that was the good soil. The Bible says these people received the seed by doing six things. They **listened to the Word, and in so doing gained faith because faith comes from hearing the Word. They held it fast through meditation, and had an honest and good heart, which simply means they were real, genuine, and sincere about their triumphs and faults.** They bore fruit (Galatians 5:22-23), and they were patient while their fruit was developing. They had contrite hearts, and God dwells with those who are contrite (Isaiah 57:15). These are all mature things to do, but how can someone who is immature understand these concepts?

This is why I believe immaturity is plaguing the church. So how do you get someone who is immature, has been saved for years, who believes they truly know God, to understand that he or she is walking in deception?

In the church today we throw seed into various grounds, but we never really tell people how to receive it. We sow, but because the people don't continue to water it, the seed never reaches their heart and brings about change.

Thus, we become forever stuck in the same cycle. Christians who have been saved for 50 years and read the Bible everyday are still unable to recognize the difference between the flesh and the Spirit in their day-to-day responses.

In some board meetings at churches, instead of caring about the souls that are being saved, the members grumble and complain about how much money the church is missing and celebrate how much money the church has made. When it's time to pray, these people are often too busy and view prayer as insignificant (even though they may talk about how important it is). Oftentimes, they elevate visions higher than the Word. They may see dreams from God as secondary to their personal opinions, or even believe that people don't receive dreams from God.

To some, nothing is demonic, or everything is demonic; Satan is powerless or Satan is to be feared; deliverance is for third world nations and Americans are too civilized to be possessed; medicine is the answer without question and it's okay if a Christian visits a medicine man. They live in a Christian dichotomy: half of their actions are from the counsel of the flesh and half from the Spirit.

Pastors have competed with me because they were comparing their ministry to mine even though we were on the same team; churches that have been prejudiced, sexist, scornful, scoff, slander, and have incorporated bylaws that exalt heresay above the Word of God. But I'm not the only one. Countless people have had the same thing happen to them and much worse.

Why does this keep happening? Of course, I believe the mastermind behind all of this is the devil, but our church system at large has become conducive to satanic operations.

CHAPTER 9

The Church System

Most churches operate like a worldly business. As a matter of fact, I've had board members explain to me why they think that a business model for a church would benefit the church. **Many believers have bought the lie that making money is the goal and souls are an afterthought.** All this is fueled by the hierarchy in our churches.

Many times, people are placed in power based on their life experience instead of their encounters with God. I've been on church boards where people didn't even know they were elders, and they didn't know what their biblical responsibility was either. It would be like me joining a basketball team and never have played basketball before but I'm on the team because I'm tall.

Now, I know you may look at my age and how long I've served in ministry and think, "you haven't been in ministry that long". This is why I took the time to interview ministers who have been ministering for years. I asked them about their experiences with church boards, and each one shared their encounters with immaturity. I asked them all these four questions:

- How long have you been pastoring?
- During your years of pastoring, would you say you had church boards that were spiritually mature?
- Would you say that the church board knew the gospel?
- Are there examples of immaturity on the church board that you could possibly elaborate on?

Here's one response from a pastor that truly spoke to the core of the issue. He has been in ministry for 33 years, and some of what he has experienced will surprise you:

I started pastoring as a lead pastor in 1991. Before that I was a youth pastor for about five years part- time or full-time with very little pay.

*Church boards are a mixed bag. I have pastored three churches as a lead pastor and will obviously leave off names and even churches in this answer. There is always a mix of maturity levels in the boards that I have worked with. I would say that one of the greatest problems with church boards is that they **tend to think in terms of serving on any type of community board and the church board as being the same.***

*They have a hard time balancing the spiritual and the practical on a church board because on any community board they only have to think in the practical to be successful.** So, the answer to your question is that there have been some serving on the board always that are spiritually minded and some that are not. And there are those that at times are spiritually minded and at other times are not. You could certainly see that as **spiritual immaturity,** or you could see that as everyone is in process, if that makes sense.*

Would I say that church boards know the gospel? In a basic sense I would say yes. They know that Jesus is the only way of salvation, and that man is a sinner and needs a savior. Some, over the years of pastoring, have not known much more than that though. I had one member at one time that

admitted that he had never read the Bible and only knew a very small amount of the Bible even though he had attended church for years.

I could give you a lot of stories. The first church I pastored I had to dismiss a church business meeting one night because two board members were at the point of a fist fight over some small matter. ***Certainly immaturity.*** *In that same church there was a time for election of a new member and the church rejected my nominee, who was a mature believer, in favor of a new believer.*

Shortly thereafter, that new member circulated a position to have me removed as pastor. I chose not to fight and resigned. ***I was making $300 a month at that church and God had done incredible financial miracles for them, but when I asked for a raise, this same board member stated that I made more money than him. He was unemployed.***

There were a lot of times that there was no vision on the part of the board. We missed an opportunity to buy a house and property for $20,000 because of no vision on the part of a board. ***Often, the board is very limited by what they see rather than free to operate by faith. I believe in counting that cost but I also believe there is a time to step out by faith.***

Even when worldly companies hire people, they don't settle for just anyone. Why do we, when we're supposed to be accountable to an eternal God? The Bible says that the harvest is plenty but the laborers are few, and that we should **pray** that the God of the harvest may send laborers into His harvest field (Matthew 9:37).

In more times than not, though, we do not truly pray. We allow our bylaws to govern our every decision instead of the word of God. **If we're not careful, we can get to a place where we scoff at God's confirmation and love people's adoration.** Our measure of how well a church is doing is not always based on how big the offering is.

In our culture, we've also isolated pastors by allowing them to operate on their own. A pastor was not created to lead alone. Timothy had Paul, Titus had Paul, and so forth. What we've done, however, is elevated one man so high that many times they fall. In many cases, this can open the door for pastors to become domineering, controlling, or prideful. Not all pastors are like that, but when we leave pastors on their own island, these temptations become enticing. **My hope is to alleviate the pressures that come with the modern-day view of pastoring.**

Here is a list of statistics about pastors in the church:

- 13% of active pastors are divorced.

- 23% have been fired or pressured to resign at least once in their careers.

- 25% don't know where to turn when they have a family or personal conflict or issue.

- 25% of pastors' wives see their husband's work schedule as a source of conflict.

- 33% felt burned out within their first five years of ministry.

- 33% say that being in ministry is an outright hazard to their family.

- 40% of pastors and 47% of spouses are suffering from burnout, frantic schedules, and/or unrealistic expectations.

- 45% of pastors' wives say the greatest danger to them and their family is physical, emotional, mental, and spiritual burnout.

- 45% of pastors say that they've experienced depression or burnout to the extent that they needed to take a leave of absence from ministry.

- 50% feel unable to meet the needs of the job.

- 52% of pastors say they and their spouses believe that being in pastoral ministry is hazardous to their family's well-being and health.

- 56% of pastors' wives say that they have no close friends.

- 57% would leave the pastorate if they had somewhere else to go or some other vocation they could do.

- 70% don't have any close friends.

- 75% report severe stress causing anguish, worry, bewilderment, anger, depression, fear, and alienation.

- 80% of pastors say they have insufficient time with their spouse.

- 80% believe that pastoral ministry affects their families negatively.

- 90% feel unqualified or poorly prepared for ministry.

- 90% work more than 50 hours a week.

- 94% feel under pressure to have a perfect family.

- 1,500 pastors leave their ministries each month due to burnout, conflict, or moral failure.[1]

How do we solve this seemingly huge problem on our hands? Well the board must be completely disassembled unless we still want to run the church like a business.

I wouldn't even use the term board anymore; I would change it to something like Council. I see the concepts of "Councils" in the Bible (Proverbs 24:6 and 15:22) are good examples. Unlike the board members whom we have come to call leaders at times, the early church had a council of elders and deacons.

Having elders and deacons instead of just a "board" helps divide the job the right way. In Acts chapter 6 it was brought to the Apostles' attention that some of the widows and the unfortunate were being neglected. The apostles though knew that their role was to provide spiritual food, yet we still need to also eat physically so they said this,

"...pick out from among you seven men of good repute, full of the Spirit and of wisdom, whom we will appoint to this duty. But we will devote ourselves to prayer and to the ministry of the word." And what they said pleased the whole gathering, and they chose Stephen, a man full of faith and of the Holy Spirit, and Philip, and Prochorus, and Nicanor, and Timon, and Parmenas, and Nicolaus, a proselyte of Antioch. These they set before the apostles, and they prayed and laid their hands on them" (Acts 6:3-6).

These men had to have great relationships with the people around them, good repute, and full of the Spirit. To be full of the Spirit you can't be full of yourself, so this means they had an intimate relationship with the Holy Spirit, they had the fruits of the Spirit (Galatians 5:22-23) and they operated in the gifts of the Spirit. Full of wisdom, Proverbs states that the fear of God is the beginning of wisdom; in the book of James, James makes a clear differentiation between Godly wisdom and worldly wisdom (James

3:13-18). Full of wisdom does not necessarily mean that they were simply practical. It means they conducted themselves with high integrity their lifestyle flowed from putting God first.

These men were not just people in the congregation voted upon through a secret ballot. Secret voting ballots work best when people's motives are aligned with the word of God. Paul states this when speaking to the church in Corinth:

"But we have renounced disgraceful, underhanded ways. We refuse to practice cunning or to tamper with God's word, but by the open statement of the truth we would commend ourselves to everyone's conscience in the sight of God" (2 Corinthians 4:2).

I believe it's easy to be underhanded when we vote secretly for people in the Church. What I mean is it can make it very appealing to some to vote not based on conscience or conviction but favoritism and performance.

In the Scriptures, the men and women who were chosen in these positions of leadership were people whose lives proved them deserving of the position that was being offered to them. **Voting is not the final say but the conviction and direction of the Holy Spirit as it was and should be.** Paul goes on to expound on the role of a deacon in 1 Timothy chapter 3:8-14. He states that

Deacons likewise must be dignified, not double-tongued, not addicted to much wine, not greedy for dishonest gain. They must hold the mystery of the faith

with a clear conscience. And let them also be tested first; then let them serve as deacons if they prove themselves blameless. Their wives likewise must be dignified, not slanderers, but sober-minded, faithful in all things. Let deacons each be the husband of one wife, managing their children and their own households well. For those who serve well as deacons gain a good standing for themselves and also great confidence in the faith that is in Christ Jesus.

There are a lot of things Paul talks about here that I believe as a church we've compromised on. The reason we have done this, I believe, has to do with verse 10: *"And let them also be tested first; then let them serve as deacons if they prove themselves blameless."* Many problems arise if we don't deal with them before we allow people to serve in leadership positions, such as elders and deacons, in the Body of Christ. Otherwise, by the time we realize that they have major issues such as slandering, alcoholism, and greed, or that they have no understanding of the gospel whatsoever, it's too late--we've already given them a position of power. Instead of them being co-laborers, they unknowingly become roadblocks.

Many churches split because leaders don't test those whom they are putting into leadership. The Bible says that those in leadership will be judged more strictly (James 3:1). Since this is true, one would think we wouldn't be so quick to appoint any and every one into a role of leadership because in so doing, we are actually setting them up for failure.

Tho term "deacon" in Greek is *diakonos*, which means servant or minister.[2] I've never seen the concept of a Christian volunteer in the Bible, yet many churches adhere to this. The term Christian volunteer is what's used by believers in some cases to indicate they are only responsible for the work they do to a certain extent; beyond this extent it is out of their hands. So, when they feel frustrated with the position, they are placed in they can just say "I'm just a volunteer" and feel justified for leaving the pastor dry. **The reality is that if we as leaders don't explain what it means for someone to be in leadership before they become a leader, they never truly consider what they are signing up for.**

The next part of the counsel is the elders. As previously stated, most boards don't truly know what the requirements are for being an elder or that members of the board are elders unless it's used otherwise. This is what Paul in 1 Timothy states as the Stipulations for anyone wanting to be an elder:

"The saying is trustworthy: If anyone aspires to the office of overseer, he desires a noble task. Therefore an overseer must be above reproach, the husband of one wife, sober-minded, self-controlled, respectable, hospitable, able to teach, not a drunkard, not violent but gentle, not quarrelsome, not a lover of money. He must manage his own household well, with all dignity keeping his children submissive, for if someone does not know how to manage his own household, how will he care for God's church? He must not be a recent convert, or he may become puffed up with conceit and fall into the condemnation of the devil. Moreover, he must be well thought of by outsiders, so that he may not fall into disgrace, into a snare of the devil" (1 Timothy 3: 1-7).

In the previous chapters, I shared a story about Jimmy and Sadee. Both Jimmy and Sadee faced pastors whose lives were not reflecting this passage. In Jimmy's case, the elder in charge of keeping the pastor accountable did not truly know what his role was, so he sided with the pastor even though it clearly states in 1 Timothy 3:3 that an overseer must be "...not violent but gentle" and that he should "manage his household well".

In Sadee's situation, the pastor/professor clearly could not manage his own household well (1 Timothy 3:4). The signs were there, but he was the head of his board at church and other board members did not really hold him accountable to the qualifications of an overseer. This made for a detrimental combination. How different could this situation have gone if this man was confronted with the Word of God, especially if the people confronting him knew how to properly hold the pastor accountable? Better yet, what if the Christian school knew how to recognize God's warning, even if it was brought to their attention through a human being?

I've sat down at church board meetings where elders could not discern what the will of God was on a regular basis. When it would come time to pray for people, some elders would just sit back instead of participating in praying. The Bible states In James 5:14

"Is anyone among you sick? Let him call for the elders of the church, and let them pray over him, anointing him with oil in the name of the Lord."

Most elders do not even show up for prayer meetings. There were times where someone asked God for confirmation and He did it, even though it was near impossible and God confirmed it, yet, the elders did not keep their commitment to God.

The reality is there are some elders who have been placed as deacons and some deacons who have been placed as elders. There is a distinct difference between the two. An elder's job is to be part of the spiritual pillars of the church: preach, teach, pray, safeguard the sheep, and stand against false doctrines (1 Timothy 5:17, Titus 1:7, 1 Peter 5:1-2, 1 Timothy 3:2, 2 Timothy 4:2, Titus 1:9, Acts 20:17; Acts 28-31).

A deacon's job is to help facilitate the heart of God through natural means, such as maintaining repute with the community, taking care of the widows and the destitute, and distributing food amongst the congregation (Acts 6:3-6, 1 Timothy 3:8-14). **Biblically speaking, elders work with the spiritual, and deacons make the spiritual practical. When you get these two jobs mixed up and nobody knows their biblical responsibilities, it can open the door for chaos and confusion.**

CHAPTER 10

Worship or Praise

The immaturity we see in the church, though, is not limited to just the board members. It's evident in every area of the church. Another area that has been affected is worship. **There are countless ways people seek to worship God, and as long as it's biblically grounded, it should be universally accepted.** So what does the Bible have to say about worship?

The first time the word worship is used in English, in the Bible, is in Genesis 22:5. Abraham and Sarah have been called out by God to follow Him. Sarah is barren, but God promises them a child and the promise comes to pass. Years later, however, God tells Abraham to take his son, his only son through Sarah, and sacrifice him on the mountain top.

Before Abraham gets up the mountain, he tells his servants who were with him and his son, *"'...Stay here with the donkey; I and the boy will go over there and worship and come again to you.'"* This statement is profound.

Knowing very well that God spoke to him to sacrifice his son, Abraham connects his act of obedience with worship. God stopped Abraham right before he sacrificed his son. He was testing him to see if he loved God for the promise or for who God was.

I want to make mention here that not every trial that arises in our life is from the enemy. In Judges we read about a God who allowed the enemies of Israel to be left for a purpose.

"Now these are the nations that the Lord left, to test Israel by them, that is, all in Israel who had not experienced all the wars in Canaan. It was only in order that the generations of the people of Israel might know war, to teach war to those who had not known it before" (Judges 3:1-2).

Sometimes our tests come from God Himself, and His testing refines and defines us.

Understanding this story and Abraham's response is crucial to knowing what worship really is. When God told Abraham to sacrifice his only son with Sarah, Abraham did not complain; he responded with faith. He saddled up his donkey and grabbed his son and servants and headed for the mountain.

There were no instruments and no songs, just obedience. So when we obey God we are worshiping Him. In Romans 12:1 it says

"I appeal to you therefore, brothers, by the mercies of God, to present your bodies as a living sacrifice, holy and acceptable to God, which is your spiritual worship."

Worshipping God goes beyond singing to God. It is a lifestyle, it is daily responding to God, it is loving God and loving your neighbor. Therefore, when we say things at church like "it's time for worship," I believe it can be a hindrance to others who may not understand that worship should be a habit. It's important to always clarify what we mean.

In the Bible Jesus says that by our words we will be justified, and by our words we will be condemned (Matthew 12:37). **Words matter to God; they also should matter to us. It's important to describe things the right way or else people may take things the wrong way.** Instead of saying "It's time to worship," we can say something like, "It's time to praise God."

Even within praise there are so many ways to praise. When the Bible mentions "praise," such as in the Psalms or other places, it means something more. There are seven words in Hebrew that can help us better describe and educate the congregation and the world on what praise is.

First, we have the word *halal*. Hallelujah comes from the word halal. Halal means "boasting to the point of looking foolish."[1] This refers to one making a show of it.

A good example of a verse is Psalms 48:1, "Great is the Lord and greatly to be praised." Even though it just says "praise" in English, it's the word halal. **In other words, God's greatness should lead us at times to boast on him to the point of looking foolish, not just in secret, but in public as well.**

Growing up, I remember when I'd go to church and see people with their hands up. I never understood why they did this. However, I learned that there are countless places in the Bible that instruct us to lift up our hands towards God. In Hebrew, the word that reflects lifting one's hands towards heaven is *yadah*.

Yadah means much more than just lifting one's hands, though. **It takes on a connotation of surrender and confession. When someone lifts their hands up, they are surrendering their life to God and declaring that He alone is their hope, joy, love, patience and so forth.** A good example can be found in Psalm 30:9: "What profit is there in my death, if I go down to the pit? Will the dust **praise (Yadah)** you? Will it tell of your faithfulness?"

The next Hebrew word for praise is *todah*. Todah means to sing praises to God together as a unit, in harmony. God did not call us to live in isolation, we are called to live life as a community. Todah is so important for the church body to stay in unity because it causes us to acknowledge that God's sacrifice is not just for us, but for our neighbor as well.

The Psalmist puts it this way:

"These things I remember, as I pour out my soul: how I would go with the throng and lead them in procession to the house of God with glad shouts and songs of **praise (todah)***, a multitude keeping festival." (Psalms 42:4)*

Keeping in step with this concept is another word in Hebrew for praise, *shaback*. Shaback is a loud adoration and a joyful-to-overwhelming attitude, testifying about what God has done.

This is one of the few words that is not just translated as the word "praise" in English. Psalm 32:11 says *"Be glad in the LORD, and rejoice, O righteous, and* **shout for joy (shaback)***, all you upright in heart!"*

Another word for praise in Hebrew is barak. To *barak* the Lord is to express an attitude of love, submission, and trust through the act of kneeling. It's a position and expression of continually giving place to God. Growing up, I remember my mom taking us to church. **While there, I would see these older people kneeling before God, and their devotion would stir up emotions in me deeper than the ocean.**

When we read the Psalms in English, the word barak translates in certain instances to the word "bless." Psalm 34:1 is a good example: *"I will **bless (barak)** the LORD at all times; His praise shall continually be in my mouth."*

Many people who were born before the 70's can recall a time when the church was not a big fan of instruments. Some churches today will still admittedly speak out against using instruments to praise God. Yet the Bible speaks the contrary to this way of thinking.

The Bible contradicts this. In Hebrew, there is actually a word that instructs one to praise God with instruments, and that's the word *zamar*. Zamar means to sing music and make music. When one is playing the drums or playing the guitar in the church, it is a zamar to God. Psalms 57:7-8 displays an example of zamar:

"My heart is steadfast, O God, my heart is steadfast! I will sing and make melody! Awake, my glory! Awake, O harp and lyre! I will awake the dawn!"

God can move through the instruments used. David's life is a testament to this. After Saul disobeys God's instructions to him through the prophet Samuel in 1 Samuel 15, an evil spirit is sent from God to torment him. **God is not the author of evil but, when God is absent darkness Is present.**

"And whenever the harmful spirit from God was upon Saul, David took the lyre and played it with his hand. So Saul was refreshed and was well, and the harmful spirit departed from him." (1 Samuel 16:23)

The act of playing the lyre is zamar, and through David's zamar, the evil spirit left.

The seventh word for praise in Hebrew is *tehillah*. It's similar to the word halal and means to boisterously and foolishly dance before the Lord by singing out loud. There are some churches that are completely silent when praise starts-nobody says anything. Although there are times to be silent in the presence of God, for anyone to say that silence is the only method of praise is not scriptural.

Tehillah is found in Psalm 100:4: *"Enter his gates with thanksgiving, and his courts with **praise (tehillah)**! Give thanks to him; bless his name!"*

These are not the only words that express praise in Hebrew, but they are the ones that explain the depth of what the psalmist is saying. Considering these seven words, it is important for the church to adequately understand and be able to explain praise and not just call it worship. **Truly praising God is part of worshipping God, but worshipping God is not just praising him through songs and instruments; it is a lifestyle.**

How then are we supposed to praise God? Paul explains this in Colossians 3:16:

"Let the word of Christ dwell in you richly, teaching and admonishing one another in all wisdom, singing psalms and hymns and spiritual songs, with thankfulness in your hearts to God."

Paul begins this verse by making sure that one understands the need for the Word of God to dwell in an individual. It's from this that he states we must teach and admonish (correct) each other in all wisdom. Continuing with this thought, he states three different ways to sing to God, "singing psalms and hymns and spiritual songs." This is anchored with the last part of the verse that says "...with thankfulness in your hearts to God."

What is the difference between psalms, hymns, and spiritual songs? **Psalms tell a story of His glory, hymns give him all the glory, and spiritual songs reveal his glory.**

As we admonish each other to better address praise in our churches, many areas of immaturity will diminish. People will be able to truly harness what it means to praise God, how to praise Him, and why we praise Him. Also, worship will no longer be seen as a time when instruments are playing, and the lights are dimmed; it will be seen as a way of life.

CHAPTER 11

Maturing in How We Decipher God's Word

In February of 2015, my wife and I moved from New York City to Montana. We came to help a pastor friend who was leading a congregation in Cut Bank, Montana.

Montana was a whole new world for me. Having graduated from a high school that had 2,500 people in Colorado, it was a culture shock moving to a town with only 3,000 people. But the biggest shock to my system was living next to a Native American reservation.

Browning is the name of the Blackfeet Native American reservation that was only about 32 miles West of Cut Bank. Being so close to the reservation had affected the demographics of Cut Bank. According to World Populations, 32% of the population of Cut Bank is Native.[1]

This meant that on a day to day basis, I would get to rub shoulders with many Native Americans. Furthermore, as time went on, our church built a great relationship with another church in Browning called Four Winds Assemblies of God. This furthered my interactions with the Native Americans.

In trying to speak to Native Americans about Jesus, they would always mention that He's the "white man's savior." Their understanding of this Jesus came from the "white men" (settlers) who first came to America. Many of them didn't present the gospel the right way to the Native Americans. They subjugated them, committing unbelievable heinous acts of violence and rape against them, stripping them entirely of their culture, dignity, and language. And the worst part of it all was that they did all these acts in the name of Jesus.

The effects of them being Biblically illiterate, has created major barriers between the Gospel of Jesus Christ and many of the Native Americans even to this very day. I believe if these settlers knew how to decipher the word of God maturely, then many, if not all, of the atrocities could have been avoided.

Unfortunately, Biblical illiteracy is not just a problem of the past. "Almost nine out of 10 households (87 percent) own a Bible, according to the American Bible Society, and the average household has three."[2] Yet, when comes to reading their Bibles a very small percentage actually do. Lifeway did research on 1,000 individuals asking them questions about Biblical literacy these were some of the results:

"One in five Americans, LifeWay Research found, has read through the Bible at least once. That includes 11 percent who've read the entire Bible once, and 9 percent who've read it through multiple times. Another 12 percent say they have read almost all the Bible, while 15 percent have read at least half.

About half of Americans (53 percent) have read relatively little of the Bible. One in ten has read none of it, while 13 percent have read a few sentences. 30 percent say they have read several passages or stories."

This survey that lifeway did however did not even ask "how many people study the Word of God?" Could you imagine how much lower the percentage would be if the question had to do with studying the Word of God?

Reading it is one thing but to truly understand what the text says one must study the Word. Today in society everyone has an interpretation for what a verse in the Bible says. But is this the way we rightly divide the Word of God?

If anyone takes Hermeneutics, that is the method for studying ancient manuscripts, one would find out that there are rules to coming to a sound interpretation of a Biblical text. Let's look at two passages and try to see how we can best ascertain the accurate interpretation of these texts.

The first verse we are going to assess is John 11:35 this is one of the shortest verses in the Bible and it simply says, "Jesus wept." If I were to say Jesus wept to show that God cries, would I be accurately interpreting this passage?

There is a truth in there, but this is not the purpose of Jesus weeping. The reason Jesus wept, some would say, is because of the unbelief, while others would say it's because of compassion, while again some might say Lazarus's death precipitated the tears.

How do you find out why this is really happening? Normally this process takes several pages. I've written a 21-page paper over one verse. For the sake of this book, however, I'm going to summarize the process. To get a better understanding of how to interpret Scripture one can read *Grasping God's Word: A Hands-On Approach to Reading, Interpreting, and Applying the Bible,* by J. Duvall and J. Hays.

First one must pray. Ask God to open the eyes of your heart so you may see the truth. Second, find out who the Author is. Then, the date when this was written because it will give you a better understanding of the culture. Read the whole book then reread the whole passage. One of the reasons why people take scripture out of context is they do not read it in context.

This is called Interpretive Analysis; you're analyzing the passage so you can better understand the purpose. While you're doing this, look for clues that might direct you to the right conclusion. After this, know your audience. John was writing to specific people with a specific culture.

Next you find the key word in the verse, "wept." When you get the word, you need to know what it means in its original language. Since this is the Gospel of John, the original writing is in Greek.

dakruó: to weep

Part of Speech: Verb

Short Definition: I shed tears, weep

Definition: I shed tears, weep.[3]

Okay so, looking at the Greek root we find out that wept means, weeping silently. So, he is literally crying. But why is He crying?

Now you can cross reference which means you search the Bible for different verses that relate to this one. There is a saying that the Bible interprets the Bible. This simply means if you cannot confirm it somewhere else in scripture there is a high chance it's your imagination.

And when he drew near and saw the city, he wept over it, saying, "Would that you, even you, had known on this day the things that make for peace! But now they are hidden from your eyes. For the days will come upon you, when your enemies will set up a barricade around you and surround you and hem you in on every side and tear you down to the ground, you and your children within you. And they will not leave one stone upon another in you, because you did not know the time of your visitation" (Luke 19:41-44).

Isaiah 53

Who has believed what he has heard from us?

And to whom has the arm of the Lord been revealed?

For he grew up before him like a young plant,

and like a root out of dry ground;

he had no form or majesty that we should look at him,

and no beauty that we should desire him.

He was despised and rejected by men;

a man of sorrows, and acquainted with grief;

and as one from whom men hide their faces

he was despised, and we esteemed him not.

Surely he has borne our griefs

and carried our sorrows;

yet we esteemed him stricken,

smitten by God, and afflicted.

But he was pierced for our transgressions;

he was crushed for our iniquities;

upon him was the chastisement that brought us peace,

and with his wounds we are healed.

All we like sheep have gone astray;

we have turned—every one—to his own way;

and the Lord has laid on him

the iniquity of us all (53:1-6).

Now let's see what the commentaries have to say about this verse. Commentaries are scholarly works of individuals or groups of people who have ineptly researched the scriptures verse by verse and some of them word by word. The one I'm going to be using is a free one online written my Matthew Henry about John 11:35.

"Christ's tender sympathy with these afflicted friends, appeared by the troubles of his spirit. In all the afflictions of believers he is afflicted. His concern for them was shown by his kind inquiry after the remains of his deceased friend. Being found in fashion as a man, he acts in the way and manner of the sons of men. It was shown by his tears. He was a man of sorrows and acquainted with grief. Tears of compassion resemble those of Christ. But Christ never approved that sensibility of which many are proud, while they weep at mere tales of distress, but are hardened to real woe. He sets us an example to withdraw from scenes of giddy mirth, that we may comfort the afflicted."[4]

In conclusion Jesus wept because his friends were weeping for their brother who died. **He shows us God's compassion; He truly can relate to us.** Furthermore, this shows us that Jesus was fully man and fully God. He had sympathy for humanity.

Verses have one interpretation but different applications. Now that we've done some of the work and researched the scriptures we can confidently say, although this is not the reason Jesus wept, **"through Jesus weeping we know that God also cries."**

The second passage is about Thomas doubting Jesus. The passage is found in John chapter 20 verse 24-29. We all talk about it in our churches, we've even dubbed him "doubting Thomas." But why is it that Thomas did not believe? Can we truly, definitively know why he doubted or are we just left with speculations?

Let's use our tools of interpretation to see if we can accurately know why Thomas doubted. First, who is the author? The author of the Gospel of John according to many scholars is John the beloved, brother of James, Jesus' cousin. One can acquire this information by looking at many different commentaries.

Secondly, who is he writing to? The audience is the Jews and Gentiles during the Roman occupation of what we know of today as Israel/Palestine. What's the purpose of the book of the Gospel of John? The purpose of the book of John is regeneration.

After this, one must read the whole Gospel because the entirety of the Gospel must be understood as one letter. There has to be an understanding that verses and chapters were not in the original text so sometimes as readers we can miss out on the meat of the passage because we believe the idea stopped when the chapter did.

As one finishes reading the book, they should get an understanding of the purpose behind what the author had written. Now one can visit the whole chapter where the verses are situated and read through it seeing if there are any situational clues.

Next, check and see if there are any other coinciding books. Since it's part of the Gospel and we know that there are four books of the Gospel, maybe there will be more clues in the other Gospels. All four of the Gospels mention Thomas but this specific situation is only alluded in Matthew 28:17 where it states, "And when they saw him they worshiped him, *but some doubted."*

Aside from Matthew, no other Gospel covers this event like the Gospel of John. Now let's check what commentaries have to say about why Thomas doubted. Many of the commentaries agree on the notion that Thomas wavered in his faith but not too many say why? Some do talk about human nature "seeing is believing" but is there more to the story?

Here are the verses surrounding the story of him doubting although the word doubt is not mentioned here the act is clearly highlighted when he states, *"'Unless I see in his hands the mark of the nails, and place my finger into the mark of the nails, and place my hand into his side, I will never believe" (John 20:25).*

John writes in the verses before Thomas doubts,

"On the evening of that day, the first day of the week, the doors being locked where the disciples were for fear of the Jews, Jesus came and stood among them and said to them, 'Peace be with you.' When he had said this, he showed them his hands and his side. Then the disciples were glad when they saw the Lord. Jesus said to them again, 'Peace be with you. As the Father has sent me, even so I am sending you.' And when he had said this, he breathed on them and said to them, 'Receive the Holy Spirit. If you forgive the sins of any, they have forgiven them; if you withhold forgiveness from any, it is withheld.' Now Thomas, one of the twelve, called the Twin, was not with them when Jesus came" (19-24).

The purpose of the Gospel of John is regeneration. This purpose is interwoven throughout the whole book. Could this be something John is speaking about here as well? Verse 22 states *"And when he had said this, he breathed on them and said to them, 'Receive the Holy Spirit...'"*

When Jesus says this is there any other place, we can find an event similar to this in the Bible? The answer is yes if we were to do an in-depth study, we would find several times; from Numbers 11 to Joel chapter 2 and some of the other prophets, where God puts his spirit or indicates He will be putting His Spirit in humanity.

But for the sake of time we are going to focus on one that many people say corresponds to this situation. There is an argument that states what John was writing here is the same as what Luke wrote about in Acts chapter 2. Let's look at what Luke wrote:

> *"When the day of Pentecost arrived, they were all together in one place. And suddenly there came from heaven a sound like a mighty rushing wind, and it filled the entire house where they were sitting. And divided tongues as of fire appeared to them and rested on each one of them. And they were all filled with the Holy Spirit and began to speak in other tongues as the Spirit gave them utterance" (1-4).*

As well-meaning as the people who are arguing this statement may have been, I believe there is a clear thing that they missed. In Acts 2, they were all in one place, but in John 20, Thomas was not there. This clearly nullifies the statement that these events are the same. What does this mean for us as readers of the word and more than this, those who are studying the Scriptures deeply?

It means when Jesus breathed on them and said "receive the Holy Spirit" it was not a baptismal situation but a regenerative one. If this is true and Thomas was not there when this event took place, then one could conclude that Thomas doubted Jesus' Resurrection in part because he was not regenerated!

It's the Spirit of God that convinces us that Jesus is Lord. The Bible says, *"Therefore I want you to understand that no one speaking in the Spirit of God ever says "Jesus is accursed!" and no one can say "Jesus is Lord" except in the Holy Spirit" (1 Corinthians 12:3).* None of the disciples believed until they saw Jesus themselves, **it was therefore the grace of God that opened the door of belief to their hearts.**

One then cannot be mad at Thomas for not believing, no man can believe in God without the persuasion and conviction of the Holy Spirit. Why then did Jesus rebuke Thomas?

Because we are all still responsible for what we've heard. Hearing is just like seeing in the Bible. *"So faith comes from hearing, and hearing through the word of Christ" (Romans 10:17).* The witness who speaks of Christ's Resurrection has grace to impart faith in a heart that's humble. Paul states this when speaking about the importance of the witness:

"How then will they call on him in whom they have not believed? And how are they to believe in him of whom they have never heard? And how are they to hear

without someone preaching? And how are they to preach unless they are sent?

As it is written, "How beautiful are the feet of those who preach the good news!"

(Romans 10:14-15)

How is it Thomas' fault then? **I don't believe Thomas is being rebuked for not having the capability to believe, but rather for not preparing his heart to receive.**

As humans there was no way for us to get to God, so God came to us. Our job is to admit when we are struggling with believing something. What do I mean? Well Thomas could have said, "guys pray for me I'm struggling with believing what you're saying" in so doing he would have taken the humble route and God always gives grace to the humble. But instead, he proudly stated *"Unless I see in his hands the mark of the nails and place my finger into the mark of the nails, and place my hand into his side, I will never believe" (v 25).*

All in all, how we handle the word of God matters. We can maturely study God's word or immaturely take scriptures out of context. As I stated earlier, if we do not mature in how we study God's word we can hurt many people and push them away from God.

The mishandling of the Word of God is directly connected to who we believe we are or how we perceive ourselves. Therefore, if our understanding of who God made us is grounded in the truth it will help us mature in how we handle God's Word.

CHAPTER 12

The Complex Us

When I think about Christians today, I'm reminded of a toy I used to play with when I was a child. It was a box with multiple different shapes in it. The goal was to fit the blocks that you had in the right shape on the box. Triangle couldn't fit in the square and vice versa. **We as a church body are out of shape because we have gifts, but we don't know where they fit in the church. Some of us don't even realize we are gifted!**

James 1:17 says that *"Every good gift and every perfect gift is from above, coming down from the Father of lights, with whom there is no variation or shadow due to change."* **Knowing what God has gifted you with is essential in knowing your purpose.** The world often uses personality tests to be able to identify how different people are gifted. Some companies encourage their management teams to take them to make sure that people understand how to better communicate, work with each other, and where they can be best used in the company.

This should be no different for the church body. We must understand what our gifts are so we can truly know how to fellowship with each other and where God wants us to be. In the first chapter of this book, I shared about the class my professor taught that wrecked my understanding of what a missionary is. It was also in this class that my professor further went on to explain the three gifts we all operate in.

Before this class I sort of knew I had gifts, but I had no idea what they really were. My class helped me to explore the formulation of us being three and one. Just like God is three in one we also are three in one: spirit, soul, and body.

The concept of a person being three in one is nothing new, but the spiritual implication of this opened my understanding in ways I never knew existed. First Thessalonians 5:23 shows this notion clearly:

"Now may the God of peace himself sanctify you completely, and may your whole spirit and soul and body be kept blameless at the coming of our Lord Jesus Christ."

Another place in the Bible this concept is clearly discussed is in Hebrews 4:12:

"For the word of God is living and active, sharper than any two-edged sword, piercing to the division of soul and of spirit, of joints and of marrow, and discerning the thoughts and intentions of the heart."

The writer of Hebrews clearly writes that God's Word pierces "to the division of soul and of Spirit, of joints and of marrow." When he states joints and marrow, he is speaking about a person's flesh.

Each part of our nature has its own function. For example, even though I'm a man, when I get married, I'm now a husband, when I have a child, I'm now a father, and these roles all become a part of who I am. **They are separate in nature, but one in me.**

Now when God created Adam and Eve, I believe humans originally knew their identity in its entirety. They could connect with God through their spirit, surrender to His will with their soul, and use their body as an instrument of worship. But when Eve was deceived and Adam willingly sinned, they lost sight of who God created them to be.

The spirit of man immediately died, and humans were left with a body and a soul that was dying. Although the New Testament is the best place to find the concept of spirit, soul, and body, this postulation is rooted in Genesis 1:26 when God said, "Let us make man in our image, after our likeness."

Who is God talking about when He says, "Let *Us*" and again "In *Our* likeness?" To answer this, I believe one must look at the clues given in Genesis 1. First, we have the Spirit of God.

The Spirit of God is introduced to us right at the beginning of the chapter, when Moses writes, *"The earth was without form and void, and darkness was over the face of the deep. And the Spirit of God was hovering over the face of the waters." (Genesis 1:2)*

Next, we hear the voice of the Father speak, *"Let there be light" (Genesis 1:3)*. Now the Son is harder to discern but I believe when God says, "'Let there be light,' and there was light," this correlates with Jesus. The reasoning I believe this is because the luminaries (the sun, moon, and stars) were not created until the fourth day.

Jesus echoes this concept when he says, *"'I am the light of the world. Whoever follows me will not walk in darkness, but will have the light of life'" (John 8:12)*. **Not that this light in Genesis was Him per se, but that this light was a *foreshadowing* of what He would eventually be to the world.**

The source of our being is our spirit. Therefore, to be born again is to be spiritually alive. Our soul is the center of our being, and this is where our will, emotions and mind come from. The body executes what the spirit or soul dictates. The body is known for its cravings like food, water, pleasure, etc, and these are influenced by the soul and spirit.

When we are born most of us will lean either toward being "feelers" or being "thinkers". Myers Briggs, a leading company on personalities, has done research on these two personalities. When trying to differentiate between thinkers and feelers, they ask questions like, "Do you like to put more weight on objective principles and impersonal facts (thinking) or do you put more weight on personal concerns and the people involved (feeling)?"

In light of this, I firmly believe that one can divide everyone in the world into two categories; the "feelers" and the "thinkers." **Feelers also think, they just process what they think through their feelings. On the other hand, thinkers also feel yet they process their feelings through their thinking.**[1]

There is no verse that plainly says a person is a feeler or a thinker, just like there is no verse that says Jeremiah was a weeping prophet (and yet everyone explains him in that way). As I alluded to in the story of Jimmy and Sadee, the word zeal can describe a person who is more of a feeler and knowledge can allude more to a thinker.

On this subject of thinker and feeler, as I will elaborate later, there are passages and characters in the Bible that reflect a feeler and a thinker's tendencies. Proverbs 3:5-6 also address the problem with relying on your heart too heavily (feelers) or leaning on your own understanding (thinkers).

The concept of a feeler and thinker is not a perfect polarity (meaning people are not perfectly one or the other), but rather, we tend to lean towards one or the other. You may feel like you're well-balanced. It's important to remember that our interactions with one another and the environment is a true indicator of how we prefer to make decisions in the world.

This is essential to understand because although we have gifts, how each gift flows from person to person varies because of the lens we use to view the world. Take for instance Jimmy and Sadee. Jimmy was clearly a feeler who operated in the gift of faith, and he would almost always be moved by what he felt. On the other hand, Sadee was a thinker and had the gift of wisdom. She was moved by what she thought.

There is also what I would like to call "cultural personalities". **In brief, this is when you grow up in a culture that shames you incognito if you act a certain way or celebrates you publicly if you act according to what society deems acceptable.** *Mores* is a good word to describe this. Mores is "the fixed morally binding customs of a particular group." [2]

In my Congolese culture, one of our mores is we can tend to be loud. Of course, not everyone in the culture is this way, but the culture sets the tone. So, if you're a shy and quiet person in the Congolese culture, a lot of times you'll be heckled and made to conform to the culture or be isolated. But the product of this is not who you truly are; it's what the culture has shaped you to be.

The Trinity has given us a gift for each part of our nature. This does not mean we are devoid of the other gifts; rather, we are naturally inclined to flow in *certain* ones. How each person uses these gifts differs based on whether they are feelers or thinkers.

A feeler who has the gift of faith, for instance, may make the statement "I feel like God wants me to get this house." A thinker who has the gift of faith may say, "I think God has chosen this house for me." Same statement different way of processing what they are hearing God say.

Now the gifts are as follows: the gift of the Father, which is found in Romans 12:4-8, is known as the *personality* gift. Although not found in this list, one can include the gift of hospitality because there are countless places where it is highlighted throughout the Word of God (Romans 12:13; 1 Pet. 4:9; Heb. 13:2; 1 Tim. 3:2, 5:10).

The gifts of the Holy Spirit, found in 1 Corinthians 12:1-26, are known as the gifts of operation. Lastly, the gift of the Son as listed in Ephesians 2:20, Ephesians 4:11-16, and 1 Corinthians 12:27-30, are what I call the "parenting" gifts. Many know these gifts as the fivefold ministry gifts.

CHAPTER 13

The Personality Gifts: My Spirit

Dictionary.com defines personality as being "the visible aspect of one's character as it impresses others." It also says that personality is "a person as an embodiment of a collection of qualities." **One's personality has two aspects: the inward perception of themselves and outward manifestation viewed by those around them.**

Each outlook, whether it be from the individual's predisposition of themselves or from the standpoint of those around them, is inclined to be biased. Every person's perspective will be affected by either self-projections or others projecting whom an individual is. Considering this tendency for us to have a proclivity for many personalities it is imperative for individuals to honestly assess who they are through a non-biased source. Personally, the only source I've found to be truthful through and through is the Bible.

In Romans 12:3-8, Paul explains the gifts that are given by the grace of God He begins by making sure that humility is the foundation from which the gifts flow. He says,

"For by the grace given to me I say to everyone among you not to think of himself more highly than he ought to think, but to think with sober judgment, each according to the measure of faith that God has assigned. For as in one body we have many members, and the members do not all have the same function, so we, though many, are one body in Christ, and individually members one of another. Having gifts that differ according to the grace given to us, let us use them: if

prophecy, in proportion to our faith; if service, in our serving; the one who teaches,

in his teaching; the one who exhorts, in his exhortation; the one who contributes, in

generosity; the one who leads, with zeal; the one who does acts of mercy, with

cheerfulness."

Let's dissect this passage verse by verse. This chapter is a continuation of Paul's beautiful invitation to the gospel. **In the previous chapters, Paul spoke about our need for the gospel, our belonging in the gospel and the need to be reverential towards the gospel.**

In verse 3 of this passage, Paul states, "by the grace given to me I say to everyone among you…". In saying this, Paul displays that he understands that he has the authority to say what he is about to say, since God has bestowed on him this right as an apostle.[1] Keeping in step with this thought, Paul exhorts the church to walk in humility. **Paul knows that if the church cannot understand that humility must take preeminence over everything else, then no matter how gifted they may be, their gifts will be a means to an end.**

Instead of being puffed up, we're instructed to view ourselves "each according to the measure of faith that God has assigned (v. 3). The intention behind this statement is to get the church to understand that no one has all the gifts. These gifts are not the same for everyone, and they are embedded in an individual by God Himself (vv. 4-6).

These gifts are the gifts of personality, and they come from the Father. They do not change. Can one grow and mature in them and learn from others who have the other giftings on this list? Of course! But the core of who God created us to be does not change.

Additionally, Paul indicates in Romans 12:6 that these gifts are to be used according to the grace given to us. As Bob Deffinbaug states,

"Spiritual gifts are gifts of grace. 'Grace' is the root (CHARIS) on which the term 'spiritual gifts' (CHARISMATA) is built. Spiritual gifts are sovereignly given as gifts of grace."[2]

I believe these gifts can be easily seen in people in the world. Since these gifts are given by God graciously, it means we did nothing to earn or deserve them; God saw it fit to fashion each gift uniquely in our spirits.

There is a total of seven of these gifts, with each being unparalleled. The first gift Paul mentions is prophecy. Paul writes that if a person's gift is prophecy, he is to use it, "in proportion to [his] faith" (v. 6). Strong's definition of the word prophecy is "the gift of communicating and enforcing revealed truth." **The statement "in proportion to our faith" sets a healthy boundary for people with prophetic personalities. Prophetic people tend to lean on seeing things too black or white, so God's Word provides the needed balance and keeps them from being overly negative in their predispositions.**

When Paul is talking about the gift of prophecy in this context, he is not referring to someone who foretells the future. Rather, he's referencing someone who announces the truth of the Word. Since prophetic people focus more on finding truth wherever it can be found, those who have a prophetic personality tend to be at odds with people who have the gifts of mercy and encouragement. In their eyes, people who encourage and are gifted as mercy-bent can seem too gracious.

Here's an example of how a prophetic person operates: let's say someone is caught in a sin. The prophetic individual will normally see this as an opportunity to show the person the truth about sin in the Word of God, or even in life. On the other hand, the same situation when dealt with by an encourager or mercy-bent person may result in that individual's sin being overlooked. **The issue is not that one view is better than the other, but that God's view is better than personal assessments of the situation.**

In John 1:14, the Bible says that *"...the Word became flesh and dwelt among us, and we have seen his glory, glory as of the only Son from the Father, full of grace and truth."* This passage is referring to Christ, who was neither too gracious nor too truthful. He was full of both attributes, equally.

Likewise, in Revelation 19:10, John states that *"...the testimony of Jesus is the spirit of prophecy."* **One's prophetic utterance or lifestyle must demonstrate who Christ is. When people see Jesus in your actions, they will know that you have matured in your personality.**

Any of these eight gifts, when left unbalanced, can be extremely dangerous. The prophetic personality in an immature state can be very legalistic in nature. **These individuals may tend to lean more towards the law than grace.**

This is very true in my Congolese church culture that I have witnessed. There is almost this unspoken belief in some Congolese churches that those who have the prophetic personality should be dominant. **But just because one gift is seen does not mean it's more honorable than the others. Prominence should not equate to dominance.**

On the other hand, when someone with a prophetic personality is mature in their gift, meaning they are humble in the way they assess themselves, the results can be powerful. In an age where everything is excused, an uncompromising individual is exactly what the church needs.

James, the brother of Jesus, accurately reflects this personality. James was very black and white on how he perceived things, as we can see from the account of him challenging Jesus in John 7:3-5, and from his own writings in the book of James. As a matter of fact, Martin Luther was uncomfortable with the book of James. In his view, it contradicted most of Paul's writings since it spoke more about doing rather than being.[3]

CHAPTER 14

Service

The next gift that Paul addresses is the gift of service. Paul states "if service, in our serving…" (Romans 12:7). Paul is making sure that each person knows what their personality is, and the accompanying actions that go along with it. It seems also that he is exhorting people not to go outside of what God has designed you to do. In other words, if God has made you someone who has a serving personality, then don't try to steal the pulpit. **This doesn't mean you won't preach. Rather, it means you will not flourish outside of being whom God has called you to be. In Acts 6 we see Stephen, the first martyr of the church, who preached the gospel. He was a deacon (which means a servant).**

The word service comes from the Greek word *diakonia*, which means "waiting at table; in a wider sense: service, ministration."[1] **People with this type of personality are the doers. They want to get things done, and if they're healthy, they don't even care if they get the credit or not.**

Most service-oriented people's qualms are normally with their leader, also known as the administrative personality. They may view the admin as lazy, since in their eyes the administrator doesn't work but he directs and tells people what to do. Also, they may see the mercy-bent people and encouragers as apathetic because their idea of work is not the same as the one who serves.

One of the most popular verses about Jesus is, *"'For even the Son of Man came not to be served but to serve, and to give his life as a ransom for many'" (Mark 10:45).*

With any of the gifts, Jesus should be the ultimate example of how, when, and why we use the gifts.

One passage that teaches us about serving is the story of Martha and Mary, as seen in Luke 10:38-42:

"Now as they went on their way, Jesus entered a village. And a woman named Martha welcomed him into her house. And she had a sister called Mary, who sat at the Lord's feet and listened to his teaching. But Martha was distracted with much serving. And she went up to him and said, 'Lord, do you not care that my sister has left me to serve alone? Tell her then to help me.' But the Lord answered her, 'Martha, Martha, you are anxious and troubled about many things, but one thing is necessary. Mary has chosen the good portion, which will not be taken away from her.'"

Clearly, Martha has the service personality. What she is doing is not wrong, but the timing is. **This is a true example of the Gospel. We often are inclined to perform for Jesus instead of being transformed by Him.** Those who have the service personality may fall into this tendency of performing. Unbeknownst to them, they may end up elevating serving over being served.

What's interesting about this passage is that the name Martha means "lord". The reality is that there is only room for one Lord in your house. What a very fitting name given the situation! In those days a name helped to define you unless God changed it. Several times in the Old Testament the Lord had to change a person's name because it was contrary to who God called them to be (see Genesis 17:5, 17:15, 32:28, 41:45, 35:10-11; Judges 6:32; 2 Samuel 12:25).

Like Martha, we must allow God to be Lord of our lives. Furthermore, one can learn several steps to take to make sure that when you invite Jesus into your home, you give Him full control.[2]

The first step is knowing who's the boss. Martha assumes she knows what's best in the situation and that somehow Jesus is missing it. Her question is accusatory in nature: "'Lord, do you not care that my sister has left me to serve alone? Tell her then to help me'" (verse 40). She is trying to take control of the situation instead of surrendering control of the situation to Jesus.

Second thing is faith must come first. The Bible says that "... faith comes from hearing, and hearing through the word of Christ" (Romans 10:17). Because Mary sat at the feet of Jesus and listened, she gained faith.

Thirdly, true faith produces work that has eternal value. As we read later in John 12:3, we find out that Mary ends up pouring a very expensive perfume, worth a year's wages, on Jesus' feet. Why? Because she understood Jesus' value. **So, working is not bad, but putting work before God or working to gain Jesus is anti-gospel.**

Lastly, Jesus is the good portion. When we're serving God, we must not put any ministry above Jesus. If we do, it becomes a distraction. Martha was anxious and troubled about many things when all she needed was the one thing, Jesus (Luke 10:41-42).

Nothing godly should cause you to be anxious. In Philippians 4:6-7, Paul puts it this way:

"Do not be anxious about anything, but in everything by prayer and supplication with thanksgiving let your requests be made known to God. And the peace of God, which surpasses all understanding, will guard your hearts and your minds in Christ Jesus" (Philippians 4:6-7).

Anxiety will steal your prayer life, take away your ability to be thankful, and strip you of your confidence in God. It will also leave you without peace.

The person with the service personality must serve from a place of being. The goal can never be to gain Christ's approval, rather *because* you have Christ's approval. Martha was immature in her gifting. However, we only see this from hindsight. If we were in the story, could we truly tell that she was immature spiritually?

CHAPTER 15

The One Who Teaches

Have you ever been in a classroom and had a teacher who loved teaching? To this day I still remember my fourth-grade teacher, Mrs. Hill. She was one of those teachers that loved what she did.

She would always read to us in class. One book that stuck with me was *Forged by Fire* by Sharon M. Draper. It was about a young African American boy named Gerald who grew up fatherless. His mother went to jail because she left him home alone when he was three years old. After his mom got out of jail, Gerald moved in with her again and had to deal with an abusive stepdad.

As she read the story, is was the first time I could see myself in my mind as a black man. I was an African boy in a pretty much all-white school. Prior to this story, all I'd ever known in my mind were white heroes. Mrs. Hill, who was a white woman, helped me realize that black heroes existed too. Gerald, who overcame all the odds, was my hero, because I could also see a lot of myself in him.

Mrs. Hill greatly impacted my life, but I don't believe she *learned* how to be a teacher. I believe teaching had always been a part of who she was. It was her personality. Because of this, everything I remember from elementary school is what I learned in her class.

When Paul says, "...the one who teaches, in his teaching" (Romans 12:7), I can't help but think of the Mrs. Hills of the world. People who teach hardly ever get paid what they truly deserve to be paid. But to them, seeing a student succeed means they've succeeded.

The word "teach" in the Greek is the word *didáskō,* which means to "cause to learn; instruct, impart knowledge."[1]

The teacher's job is to cause others to grow by spreading the information they've learned.

But like all the other gifts, the teaching personality can be used immaturely. Many teachers can fall more in love with their material rather than people. **Knowledge can puff up an individual, while love seeks to build others up (1 Corinthians 8:1).**

A person I believe had the teaching personality in the Bible was Apollos. In Acts 18:18-28, we learn that Apollos was a Jew who came to know the Lord. The Bible states that he was an "educated man" who "knew the scriptures very well" (v. 24).

Apollos "spoke with great power" and "he taught the truth about Jesus" (v. 25). Yet the thing that I love about him the most is his willingness to learn in humility.

In Acts 18, we read about how Apollos only knew about John's Baptism (v. 25), which means he learned about Jesus through John the Baptist's ministry instead of all the teachings Jesus taught. Nowadays, most of us would be satisfied with what we know especially if we are winning new converts. Yet we read this about Apollos:

"He began to speak boldly in the synagogue. Priscilla and Aquila heard him. So they invited him to their home. There they gave him a better understanding of the way of God (Acts 18:26)."

Apollos was an educated man who was winning souls for the kingdom, yet still showed true maturity in his ability to walk in humility. The Bible says Priscilla and Aquila taught him and "gave him a better understanding" (v. 26). For a Jew to sit down and be willing to learn from a woman in that day and age speaks volumes about the meekness of Apollos.

CHAPTER 16

The One Who Exhorts

After the personality gift of teaching, Paul addresses the next gift: "the one who exhorts, in his exhortation" (Romans 12:8). Since we don't really use exhorting in our day-to-day lingo, one can exchange this word with *encourager* or *mentor*.

The word that is used here in Greek, *parakalōn*, encompasses this concept of encouragement and mentoring. The Strong's definition has at least four parts: (a) I send for, summon, invite, (b) I beseech, entreat, beg, (c) I exhort, admonish, (d) I comfort, encourage, console.[1]

There's another word that most of us have come to know that's connected to parakalōn, and it is paraklétos. The Holy Spirit is our paraclete; our advocate and comforter. Jesus says this about the Holy Spirit: "Nevertheless, I tell you the truth: it is to your advantage that I go away, for if I do not go away, the Helper will not come to you. But if I go, I will send him to you (John 16:7)". That word helper, in other translations, comforter, advocate, intercessor is the Greek word *paraklétos*, or in English, paraclete. **In other words, to truly encourage others you must know the true encourager.**

Parakalōn must be balanced, like all the other gifts. I've known people who have this gift and all they ever see in people is the good. They overlook the bad even if it is blatant. But what does it mean to admonish someone? According to the dictionary when you admonish someone you warn them sharply and even firmly.[2] It's still done from a loving heart, but it's stern.

Since our giftings greatly affect our worldview, oftentimes the encourager will tend to view the prophetic personality as mean and ill willed. They are both, however, showing an aspect of God, as long as their speech and action is full of grace and truth (John 1:14).

Sometimes we tend to make blanket statements about God. For instance, to an encourager God will never speak to anyone while He is angry. Yet we find throughout the New Testament that there were times Jesus got mad and spoke to people while he was mad (Matthew 21:12-13, Mark 11:15-18, John 2:13–16). God got mad countless times (Exodus 4:14, Psalm 7:11, 1 Kings 11:9–10; 17:18). I could list multiple scriptures; it's called righteous indignation. Psalms 7:11 states that *"God is a righteous judge, and a God who feels indignation every day."* The difference is God's anger is righteous and still full of love.

One person who personified the personality gift of encouragement was Barnabas. We are first introduced to him in Acts 4, where he sells some land to benefit the church body (Acts 4:36-37). It is here that we get why he has the name that he is given, because his real name is Joseph, but he was *"...called by the apostles Barnabas (which means son of encouragement)"* (v. 36).

As I previously mentioned, nicknames are often birthed based on *what an individual demonstrates* or *what someone projects onto a person.* Imagine with me then, the type of person Joseph was that the Apostles called him a "son of encouragement" (Acts 4:36). Barnabas knew who he was and manifested that instead of pretending to be who people wanted him to be.

Barnabas only accompanied Paul on his first missionary journey because he and Paul ended up having a sharp dispute and parted ways for a little while. Paul had three missionary journeys; the first one was recorded in Acts 13:1-15:35, the second in Acts 15:36-18:22, and the last one in Acts 18:23-21:17.

I firmly believe Paul needed Barnabas and vice versa. The Holy Spirit makes this apparent when he says this to the Apostles, *"Set apart for me Barnabas and Saul for the work to which I have called them" (Acts 13:2).* God literally called them to do ministry together.

But both had different personalities. I believe that their split was partly due to their personality differences. We read that from the beginning of their ministry, John Mark, who also is Barnabas' cousin, was with them (Acts 13:5). Sometime during their journey though, John Mark abandons or leaves them to go back to Jerusalem (Acts 13:13).

His actions didn't sit well with Paul, so when Barnabas wanted John Mark to join them again, Paul was against it (Acts 15:38). Paul viewed John as someone who deserted them while Barnabas viewed John as someone who would be instrumental to their ministry. Barnabas is seeing through his eyes of encouragement while Paul is either seeing through his leadership/prophetic personality. He appears to be very black and white on this issue.

We can infer that some level of reconciliation took place based on an accumulation of verses like 2 Timothy 4:11, where Paul asks for John Mark, and Colossians 4:10 and 1 Corinthians 9:5, where Paul addresses Barnabas in a positive light and compares him to himself. **It appears that navigating through personalities**

is hard and can oftentimes be impossible without the Holy Spirit. In this case, even Barnabas and Paul had to mature in their giftings.

CHAPTER 17

In His Generosity

While I was courting my wife, she would always get onto me because any time I saw an opportunity to give something away, I would do it without thinking. I gave away thousands of dollars, clothes, shoes, I nearly even gave my life away by jumping in front of a driver who was about to drive home drunk. At the time I thought it was heroic and even godly. When people looked at me, they would immediately think, "man he has a giving heart." But did I really?

Three years into our marriage, you can imagine that my giving under compulsion became problematic. I had become addicted, and I found it irresistible. I would give away anything and everything, including gifts my wife gave to me. It was time for a heart check.

As my wife and I talked through this issue, I started to realize that the devil had deceived me into believing that I did not deserve good things. So, when I had anything good, I gave it away because I didn't see myself as valuable. After understanding this, I realized that giving wasn't necessarily my gift, it was my coping mechanism.

Instead of leaning on giving, I should have allowed the Holy Spirit to help me cope with life. Furthermore, I needed to know that my value came from Jesus and not anything I could do. **When I give, it should not be so He *will be* pleased with me but because He is *already* pleased.** Therefore, one should only give because *"God so loved the world that He gave" (John 3:16).*

When Paul says, "the one who contributes, in generosity" (Romans 12:8), for instance, he's not talking about someone who just gives away their home in hopes to gain a heavenly home. He's talking about one who knows that they have a heavenly home, and considering this, they purposefully give. A mature giver will give in secret and will make sure that they understand where the finances are going. They never want to be coerced into giving.

A great word that truly expounds on this concept of giving is the word "generosity." The word generosity in the Greek is *eumetadotos* (yoo-met-ad'-ot-os) which means, "willingly sharing, ready to impart, generous."[1]

The fact that Paul states "the one who contributes in generosity" means one must grow into their gift of giving like any other gift. **In other words, just because your gift is giving, doesn't mean you know how to be generous. Likewise, just because someone looks generous doesn't mean their gift is giving.**

For instance, I thought I was being generous, and I even looked generous. However, my motives were off, and **what I thought was generosity actually was compulsory giving. True givers who are still maturing in their gift may seem reluctant to give at times because a true heart of generosity comes from intimacy with the Holy Spirit.**

A person who had this gift in the Bible is the Roman soldier named Cornelius. In Acts 10, we learn about his giving and the impact it had. One day, an angel of the Lord showed up to Cornelius and said to him, "*...Your prayers and gifts to the poor have come up as a memorial offering before God" (v. 4).*

Let's consider the depth of this statement. What was it about his giving that caused Heaven to notice and moved the heart of God? First, we need to observe closely who he gave to the poor. Proverbs 19:17 states, *"Whoever is generous to the poor lends to the LORD, and he will repay him for his deed."* Matthew 6:3-4 reverberates this notion: *"But when you give to the needy, do not let your left hand know what your right hand is doing, so that your giving may be in secret. And your Father who sees in secret will reward you."* **Each passage states that God will reward those who give to the needy but there is a clause; one must do it in secret and for the glory of God.** This is precisely what Cornelius did.

Secondly, Cornelius didn't just do the practical steps; he also prayed for the poor. **Anybody can take care of the poor and orphans and still not touch Heaven because their heart can be wrongly motivated. Prayer brings about the right motives and moves the heart of God.**

Lastly, it says that it was a "memorial offering before God." This indicates that his giving was more acceptable than the sacrifices of bulls or goats and it came from the heart.[2] It's important to note that Cornelius did all this before he truly knew the Lord (Acts 10:34-48).

Cornelius is a great example of a true giver. Cornelius gave for the glory of God. If he was alive today, he would not post it on social media to receive the approval of men, because his goal would be to please God.

CHAPTER 18

The One Who Leads

When I was in college, I went on a mission trip to Louisiana during Mardi Gras. I've never seen anything like it in my whole life. Streets were jammed packed with people on Bourbon Street, which is the ideal place for people who were looking to do any and everything crazy.

We partnered with a church that had a small building next to Bourbon Street. Since there were so many people, bathrooms were scarce, and people charged money to use them. To reach people with the gospel, we opened the bathroom up for people to use, free of charge.

Using the bathroom is a necessity, especially if you've been drinking like a sailor. We figured people would have no choice but to come into the church and listen to the gospel while they waited. We had a group of people prepared to talk with those who were waiting in line. Not in a weird way, but just getting to know them and hearing their stories.

Another team was doing praise and praying in between praise sets. The team I was with asked me to pray. I grabbed the mic. **In that moment, I couldn't help but think of all the brokenness that was before me. I felt like a fire came upon me, and I felt anguish.**

As I began to pray, my prayers got louder and louder and tears filled my eyes. On my mind was all the lost people who I bumped into as I was walking, or I talked to. After I finished praying, one of my friends told me a story about a man who wanted to meet me. Apparently as I was praying there was someone walking outside who happened to hear me. The man who was outside said that "he felt drawn into the building."

When the man came into the building, his eyes were fixed on me. After he sat down my friend went up to him to get his story, and without looking at my friend, he said these words that have stuck with me to this day: "I have never heard or seen such passion in my life."

What amazes me about passion is even the world recognizes it. The Bible says, *"Do not be slothful in zeal, be fervent in spirit, serve the Lord (Romans 12:11)."* **Zeal or passion is paramount for every believer, but it is even more needed if your personality gift is leading (also known as administrative)**. I believe Paul recognized this when he said, "the one who leads, with zeal" (Romans 12:8).

There have been many great leaders throughout history. Being a leader is not easy, because there are so many people watching what you say and do. It's usually not the outside pressure that destroys a leader, but what's inside of them.

Many people believe that what causes leaders to fall is pride. I actually think its insecurity. Many people who have an administrative personality try to cover up shame by seeking the praise of others. Unresolved shame can evolve into pride.

A great biblical example of someone who had an administrative gift is Peter. Peter was always taking the lead with passion, whether for good or bad. Sometimes he would proclaim Jesus was the Messiah (Matthew 16:16). Other times he would oppose Jesus and have to be rebuked by him (Matthew 16:23). You can clearly see the struggle Peter had as a leader.

The danger about leading is people will follow you, whether your intentions are good or evil. As Peter matures, a dichotomy can be seen it's like half of him wanted to be a good leader but the other half is struggling with man's approval. Seeking the approval of man is a major sign of insecurity.

Jesus, though, being full of grace and truth, sees right through Peter's man-pleasing tendencies and openly tells him, *"Truly, I tell you, this very night, before the rooster crows, you will deny me three times" (Matthew 26:34).* Accustomed to making sure he looked good in man's eyes, Peter responds by saying he would die before betraying Jesus (Matthew 26:35). This sounded good to those around him, but unknowingly, Peter was telling Jesus that He was wrong.

Jesus didn't make that statement to place guilt on Peter, but to show him just how far he was willing to go to hide his insecurities. Therefore, confession is instrumental for every believer. Confession is the path to humility. If Peter had confessed to Jesus that he was insecure and fighting for a position to be the greatest, I firmly believe he wouldn't have gone on to deny Jesus.

His insecurities that manifested through seeking the approval of men led him to do something shameful. Fortunately for him, Jesus confronted the shame immediately.

At the end of the gospel of John, Jesus has an exposing conversation with Peter. He asks Peter three times about his love for Jesus. In the Greek, the first two times Jesus asked Peter if he unconditionally loved Him, and both times Peter responded by saying he only had affection for him. As Jesus asked these questions, He also confirmed Peter's calling each time and confronted the shame of Peter's denial (John 21:15-17 New Heart English Bible).

On the third time, Jesus goes down to Peter's level and asks him if he had affection for Him. This caused Peter to be grieved. Instead of just stating he had affection for Him, this time Peter humbly admits that Jesus knows everything. He never says that he had somehow gained unconditional love for Jesus but is genuinely true to what he currently possessed towards Christ, which was just affection for Him (John 21:15-17).

It is important that we never pretend to be more than we are (Romans 12:3). In other words, confess your struggles to God. Psalm 25:3 says, *"No one who trusts in you will ever be disgraced" (ESV),* but *"disgrace comes to those who try to deceive others" (NLT).* **Pretending to be something or someone you are not is deceptive.**

After this dialogue Jesus tells Peter to follow Him. Yet Peter, still dealing with his insecurities, asks Jesus about the other disciple who was next to him. Jesus again confronts this in Peter and says, *"'...If it is my will that he remain until I come, what is that to you? You follow me!" (John 21:22).*

Peter would go on to plant many churches and save thousands, but even years after Jesus is taken up to Heaven, we still see through Paul's writings that Peter struggled with this area of man pleasing throughout his life (Galatians 2). Each time he was confronted, though, he responded in humility.

We can find hope by examining Peter's life. Peter is known as a pillar in the church (Galatians 2:9), yet he too struggled in his walk with Christ. **Too many times we allow our insecurities to get the best of us because we are ashamed of our inability to be where we believe we should be with God.** It's not our job to perfect ourselves; it's God who is perfecting us. Although Peter's administrative gift was immature initially, as he stayed humble, he eventually matured. Like Peter, maturity will eventually come into our lives if we choose to walk in humility.

CHAPTER 19

One Who Does Acts of Mercy

For most of my life, the word mercy had been a foreign concept to me. I'd heard many preachers speak on mercy, but I couldn't truly come to terms with it in my day-to-day interactions with people. I also had trouble distinguishing the difference between the two, as I perceived them to be the same thing.

One day, though, someone took the time to clearly explain to me what grace is and what mercy is. They said to me, **"grace is giving someone something they don't deserve while mercy is not giving someone who does evil the punishment they deserve."**

In other words, let's say someone were to steal and get caught and the judge were to let them go, agreeing to pay for classes to help the individual learn how not to steal. This is grace. In the same scenario, if the judge were to withhold jail time even though he deserves it, this would be mercy. Understanding grace and mercy is pivotal for a believer's walk with Christ.

Where does mercy come from? Like all the gifts, mercy flows from the heart of God. While God has some incommunicable attributes (characteristics that He doesn't share with us) like his ability to be omniscient, omnipotent, and omnipresent, mercy is a communicable attribute, as are love, peace, kindness and so forth.

Even though we share this attribute with God, our mercy barely looks like God's mercy. God's mercy is magnanimous in nature, meaning He is the only being who can forgive and forget. It is not impulsive; God chooses to have mercies as He sees fit. All of

God's merciful tendencies are well balanced within his other attributes. So balanced, in fact, that one can say God's mercies are forever and his justice will not wait forever.

Unlike Gods mercy, though, the mercy personality must mature like all the other personality gifts. As I previously mentioned, someone who has this personality may not get along well with a person with a prophetic personality. For a person who shows mercy, *"hatred stirs up strife but love covers all offenses" (Proverbs 10:12).*

This verse is very true but can be easily misused. **"Love covers all offenses" does not mean that to love is to be okay with the offense, and it doesn't mean that you don't confront the offender. It does mean love does not parade the offense in a shameful fashion and continue to bring up the offense in a condemning way.**

Most people who have a merciful personality can also tend to run themselves to the ground on the account of caring for others. This sometimes can lead to them experiencing heartache after heartache. After the heartache has run its course, showing mercy may become weakness to them, causing their hearts to grow cold.

Therefore, Paul states that the one who does acts of mercy needs to do so with cheerfulness (Romans 12:8). Mercy should flow from a heart of joy, which is a fruit of the Spirit (Galatians 5:22-23). This means that although a person may have a merciful personality, without joy, their mercy will be skewed and end in pain.

A person in the Bible whom I believe may have had a merciful personality is the prophet Jeremiah. When you read through the book of Jeremiah and Lamentations, you can't help but hear the heart of God and feel Jeremiah's pain. His task was daunting; he had to go to a people who were not going to listen and tell them to surrender to their enemies for their own good because they rebelled against God.

Because of this, he was beaten, shamed, tossed in a pit. Lamentations 3:1-10 puts it this way:

"I am the man who has seen affliction under the rod of his wrath...He has made my flesh and my skin waste away; he has broken my bone...though I call and cry for help, he shuts out my prayer."

Jeremiah poured out his pain and agony to God. He knew that God was the one who allowed these things to happen to him. Jeremiah didn't blame God, but he acknowledged his pain to Him. He understood that considering everything, God is still merciful.

"But this I call to mind, and therefore I have hope: The steadfast love of the Lord never ceases; his mercies never come to an end; they are new every morning; great is your faithfulness. 'The Lord is my portion,' says my soul, 'therefore I will hope in him'" (Lamentations 3:21-24).

What we can learn from Jeremiah is that each of us will face different trials in life that can either strengthen our personality or destroy our character. **The world will not exonerate you, no matter how perfectly you respond to what God tells you to do. Still, we shouldn't allow them or our own weakness to lose vision and abort the mission.**

What's interesting about this story is that when Jeremiah spoke to the Israelites about them surrendering to Babylon, it was the most merciful thing he could have done, even though God was judging them. Sometimes we believe mercy can't confront, but Jeremiah confronted. We also may think that mercy overlooks sin, but Jeremiah didn't overlook the sin. Instead, he showed the people how to get out of sin. Lastly, Jeremiah could have allowed his heart to be hardened. At times, he probably did struggle with being bitter, as we read in Lamentations, but he found strength when he put his hope and confidence in the Lord.

CHAPTER 20

The Gift of Hospitality

We are all called to be hospitable (Romans 12:13), just like we're all called to serve, give, and encourage one another. **But for some, hospitality isn't simply a response to the Word of God; it is a part of who God has called them to be.**

I have a sister in the Lord whom I call Mama Sarah. When I think of someone who has a gift of hospitality, her name immediately comes to mind. Whenever I visit her home, I always see or meet someone new.

She's also welcoming to strangers. In Hebrews 13:2, the writer instructs believers to *"not neglect to show hospitality to strangers, for thereby some have entertained angels unawares."* This literally means that sometimes angels may come to earth and look just like one of us. Just as Lot welcomed the two angels into Sodom, which turned out to be a blessing upon his life, we too can experience such an encounter with the supernatural if we obey what the Word says about hospitality. Of course, this shouldn't be the motivation, but it's part of choosing such a lifestyle.

Mama Sarah had to learn how to balance her gift with her husband's gift, however. Whereas she was very hospitable, her husband Ron preferred privacy. It wasn't that he didn't love people, but that he wanted to protect his family from those who would try to take advantage of them. He knew that although we should be as gentle as doves, we also need to be as wise as serpents (Matthew 10:16).

Now I'm sure Mama Sarah could have defended her gifting with countless Scriptures that deal with people being hospitable. Maybe she could have even won the argument, yet in doing so, many have lost the war.

We are not called to segregate ourselves; we must be a body. Each part of us serves a purpose and none of us should usurp power just because we believe our gifts are right. It's not always about being right, it's about admitting when we're wrong.

Being the great woman of God, she is, Mama Sarah heeded her husband's advice. She still entertains company, but now she is more balanced, and her family also has a sense of privacy in their home. **Jesus welcomed the crowds and even entertained them, but He dwelt with the twelve inside and met with the crowds outside.**

Throughout the Bible there are many people who displayed the gift of hospitality, but Priscilla and her husband Aquila stand out the most. One cannot know for sure whether they both had the gift of hospitality, or just one of them. Either way, they balanced each other well from what we read in Scripture.

We first meet Priscilla and Aquila in Acts 18 where we find them opening their home for Paul. During this time, Emperor Claudius had commanded all the Jews to leave Rome. Some believe this happened because the Pharisaical Jews were persecuting their Christian brothers and sisters, which created unrest in the land (Acts 18:1-2).

But Paul was not the only person whom Priscilla and Aquila welcomed into their home. There was another man by the name of Apollos whom Paul spoke very highly of

(1 Corinthians 1:12). Priscilla and Aquila invited him into their home as well and invested in him (Acts 18:24-26).

This dynamic duo would go onto open up their home to many more people. They would eventually have a church that met at their home (1 Corinthians 16:19). **Their willingness to be hospitable shaped men and women of God and led many to the Lord.**

To find out your personality gifts, take the Personality Gifts Test in the back of the book.

CHAPTER 21

The Gifts of Operation: My Soul

The City of Corinth was very economically stable. It was known as one of the chief commercial cities of the Roman Empire. Its location made it a natural center of commerce and transportation. Prior to being a Roman territory, Corinth was under the control of the Achaians. When they began to revolt against Rome around 146 B.C., Rome destroyed them. "After the decisive engagement at Leucopetra, on the Isthmus, the consul Lucius Mummius was able to occupy Corinth without a blow. The citizens were killed...the city itself was leveled with the ground...". [1]

Rome would later rebuild the city of Corinth, but this time it would be under Roman control. After 100 years of desolation, Corinth was rebuilt by Julius Caesar as a Roman Colony.[2] Not too long after Corinth was rebuilt, it would resume its place as one of the top cities in the world in relation to its economic stability.[3]

Although this rebuilding was good for the economy, it was not a good environment for people wanting to live morally. **In fact, Corinth was such an immoral city that people started to use the city's name as an adjective to describe people that lived immorally. Thus, the term "to get Corinthanized" was used, which "was popular Greek for 'go to the devil.'"[4]**

Aphrodite, goddess of sexual love, was reflected in the city's reputation for immorality, and many Corinthians worshipped at her temple. Her temple boasted 1,000 female prostitutes and was one of the reasons why so many people journeyed to Corinth.

Unfortunately, instead of being the light amid this darkness, the church of Corinth allowed the darkness to infiltrate their congregation. Paul hearing about this writes them a letter to address their immaturity. In 1 Corinthians 12, Paul specifically addresses the immature way they operate in the gifts. He doesn't forbid them from using the gifts, but he encourages them to not abuse them.

Each of the following gifts flows from the Holy Spirit and are only to be used by believers who surrender control of their lives to the Holy Spirit (1 Corinthians 12:1-3).

"Now there are varieties of gifts, but the same Spirit; and there are varieties of service, but the same Lord; and there are varieties of activities, but it is the same God who empowers them all in everyone. To each is given the manifestation of the Spirit for the common good. For to one is given through the Spirit the utterance of wisdom, and to another the utterance of knowledge according to the same Spirit, to another faith by the same Spirit, to another gifts of healing by the one Spirit, to another the working of miracles, to another prophecy, to another the ability to distinguish between spirits, to another various kinds of tongues, to another the interpretation of tongues. All these are empowered by one and the same Spirit, who apportions to each one individually as he wills" (1 Corinthians 12:4-11).

To better understand the gifts, one can categorize them into three classifications. There are the oral gifts (various kinds of tongues, interpretation of tongues and prophecy), the revelatory gifts (word of knowledge, word of wisdom and ability to distinguish between spirits or discernment), and the power gifts (faith, healing and working of miracles).

There are some similarities and differences between the personality gifts from the Father and the gifts of operations from the Holy Spirit. They are similar in that an individual only gets one prominent gift, thus the term "to another" repeated by Paul each time he mentioned a personality gift. They are different in how they are given and used.

While the personality gifts were given by the grace of God and each person received their lot according to the faith given them, **the gifts of operation flow from the Spirit of God and are a manifestation of one's relationship with God's Spirit** *"who apportions to each one individually as he wills" (1 Corinthians 12:11).*

The reason I believe each person has one primary gift of operation is based on the dialogue Paul has about the body following these verses. As Paul explains in 1 Corinthians 12:12-20,

"For just as the body is one and has many members, and all the members of the body, though many, are one body, so it is with Christ. For in one Spirit we were all baptized into one body—Jews or Greeks, slaves or free—and all were made to drink of one Spirit. For the body does not consist of one member but of many. If the foot should say, 'Because I am not a hand, I do not belong to the body,' that would not make it any less a part of the body. And if the ear should say, 'Because I am not an eye, I do not belong to the body,' that would not make it any less a part of the body. If the whole body were an eye, where would be the sense of hearing? If the whole body were an ear, where would be the sense of smell? But as it is, God

113

arranged the members in the body, each one of them, as he chose. If all were a single member, where would the body be? As it is, there are many parts, yet one body."

According to Paul, in relation to the gifts bestowed on each person, we all are different and yet essential to the body of Christ. But this passage is not a new train of thought; it is connected to Paul's previous conversation about the gifts given by the Holy Spirit. So, if the gift of personality is how you see the world, then the gift of operation would be how you act on what you see.

It's important to note that a person cannot love God and not love Jesus, nor can one love Jesus and not love His word, nor can one love the Holy Spirit and not love His gifts.

Jimmy and Sadee had to learn and mature in their gifts of operation. Jimmy's prominent gift from the Holy Spirit was the gift of faith. He saw things black and white like Sadee. However, while Sadee would take her time to step out, he would move as soon as he believed he heard God say go.

Sadee's gift of operation was wisdom. For Sadee if God spoke something to her, she had to assess and see how what God said could wisely be implemented. She would eventually act, but sometimes way too slow. Jimmy, on the other hand, would sometimes move way too fast.

Both had to realize that they were important to each other and no one's gift was more important, unless a particular season called for the exercise of one gift over another. In Ecclesiastes 3:1-10, Solomon speaks about the different seasons in life.

"For everything there is a season, and a time for every matter under heaven:

a time to be born, and a time to die;

a time to plant, and a time to pluck up what is planted;

a time to kill, and a time to heal;

a time to break down, and a time to build up;

a time to weep, and a time to laugh;

a time to mourn, and a time to dance;

a time to cast away stones, and a time to gather stones together;

a time to embrace, and a time to refrain from embracing;

a time to seek, and a time to lose;

a time to keep, and a time to cast away;

a time to tear, and a time to sew;

a time to keep silence, and a time to speak;

a time to love, and a time to hate;

a time for war, and a time for peace.

Seeing that there are different seasons in life, it makes more sense why a gift may be needed more in one season over another. (For more on seasons, check out *The Silent Season: What to Do When God is Silent* by Wendy Tufor Asare.)

During the season that Sadee and Jimmy showed up to Maine and God was calling them to trust Him, Sadee needed to submit her gift to Jimmy's gift because that's how God wanted them to operate.

This would be the same for Jimmy if they were in a season where God spoke to them and said you need to make wise decisions and be more practical. In a season like this, Jimmy would submit his gift of faith and give room for Sadee to operate in her gift of wisdom. **Although faith may seem like it's more important than godly wisdom, one must understand that God does not need faith, he is all knowing. In other words, His wisdom is our faith.**

Understandably, the Bible wants all of us to be wise and walk by faith, but as I will further explain, being wise is different than giving a word of wisdom, just like a gift of faith is not the same as salvific faith. So, when I say a *season of faith,* I do not mean in that season someone who operates in a gift of faith should not seek wise counsel or use wisdom in their day-to-day interactions. Similarly, in a season where God may call us to walk wisely, it doesn't mean we shouldn't step out in faith.

In connection to the way the gifts of the Holy Spirit operate, I have found that although each person has a primary gift, they may at times find it easier to flow in the other two gifts in their category. For instance, someone who has a gift of faith may find it easier to believe for miracles, and healings, and so on.

If we have one primary gift and at times we may flow within our categories, how do we go about learning or even operating in the other gifts of operation? I firmly believe humility is the key. When one gives room for others to operate in their gifts, one can learn from whoever it is that they allow to operate. Also, being willing to listen to teachings by these individuals can help you gain insight as well. In the next few

chapters, we're going to look more closely at each of the gifts of operation.

CHAPTER 22

The Oral Gifts

While I was in college, I got to experience and see the gifts of the Holy Spirit in operation frequently. One day, I was in the prayer room and there was a man of God by the name of Paul Chishala who was praying for people. On this specific day, there was an individual who came in and wanted more of God.

Brother Paul approached him and told him that he was going to pray that God's Spirit would come and that he would receive it. So, he began to pray, but not in English. To many in the room, the words that were coming out of his mouth may have sounded like gibberish, but not for me. I could understand what he was saying because he was speaking in my native language, Lingala.

He said, "Yaka ka ka ka ka, Yaka ka ka ka ka, Ma! Ma!" After he finished praying, I went to him and asked him if he spoke Lingala, and he said no. I was so blown away. In my language, "yaka" means "come". If you urgently want someone to come, you would say, "Yaka ka ka ka" and if you want someone to have something, you would say "ma."

He was speaking my language without having ever learned it. This is the gift of various kinds of tongues--the ability to speak in a foreign language supernaturally. This is not to be mistaken with speaking in tongues as the initial evidence of the Holy Spirit baptizing an individual, which is mysterious and is a direct communication with God (1 Corinthians 14:2). The difference is that the gift of various kinds of tongues is for the body of Christ, while a person's private gift of speaking in tongues is to edify themselves (1 Corinthians 14:4) and is a gift that empowers you to be a witness (Acts 1:8).

I've been in services where everyone in the service was encouraged to speak in tongues out loud. I used to join in, but the more I read 1 Corinthians 14:4, the more I realized that this is an immature way to act. **The public service should be a place where people can communicate with God in sync. Unity can make things clearer. It's hard for me to unite with someone when I don't understand what they are saying.** Plus, speaking in tongues was supposed to be a "sign not for believers but for unbelievers" (1 Corinthians 14:22).

What is the sign that Paul is talking about? Paul is quoting from the Old Testament in Isaiah 28:11-12 where God states:

"For by people of strange lips and with a foreign tongue the Lord will speak to this people, to whom he has said, 'This is rest; give rest to the weary; and this is repose'; yet they would not hear."

This was spoken from a standpoint of judgment. The sign isn't a positive sign for an unbeliever, but one that shows that God's judgment has begun.

So, I don't believe we as believers should freely speak in tongues in the presence of unbelievers unless someone interprets or the person speaking knows what they are saying, and they give an interpretation. Also, there is the rare occasions where the Holy Spirit would prompt you to do so, because unknowingly He may use you to speak in a foreign language.

Paul puts it this way: *"...the one who prophesies is greater than the one who speaks in tongues, unless someone interprets, so that the church may be built up"* (1 Corinthians 14:5). Remember that just because a great minister is doing it does not mean that's how Jesus ordained it to be done. Our mandate is to submit to the Word not to have the Word submit to us. This is maturity.

I remember the first time God used me to give a message of tongues in a service. I was in college and we were having chapel. As the praise team was singing the atmosphere changed in the room, and everyone started to cry out to God.

All of a sudden, I felt as if my stomach was on fire and the fire was moving up towards my mouth. There seemed to be a gap of silence in the service and I could feel something prompting me to open my mouth and let the fire out, so I did.

After I finished speaking in this unknown tongue I waited and the whole chapel waited. Suddenly, someone in another part of the chapel gave an interpretation. The whole place erupted with praise as God was glorified.

This does not mean every time someone gives a message of tongues; they will feel a fire in their stomach. It's important to remember that each person's personality is different, and unity in the Spirit does not mean uniformity.

There are some other things we need to keep in mind about the gift of tongues. One, the gift does not control you. Many people, when using this gift, will do it right when the worship is going on or as the pastor is preaching. This is out of order. On the other hand, many churches will not give the Holy Spirit room to move so they schedule every single minute without giving the gifts a place to operate. This is out of order as well.

True, godly order is being prepared while still being flexible and leaving room for the Holy Spirit to operate. Sometimes, silence shows reliance while ambiance can equate to defiance. We don't always have to be loud to get God's attention.

CHAPTER 23

Interpretations of Tongues

Having been raised in the Congo, I grew up speaking French and Lingala. **Both languages have their own rules and idioms influenced by the culture mores, and I found this to be the same when it came to learning English.**

Sometimes, a gesture in Lingala would take a whole sentence to be able to express correctly in English. Other times, one word could do the job. **Interpretations can't always be translated word-for-word, which is evidenced by the variety of Bible translations we currently have. Some Bible interpretations lean more on the word for word end of the spectrum while others lean more toward thought for thought.**

The example I like to use to illustrate this point comes from the movie *The Lion King*. When Simba meets Timon and Pumba, they teach him the phrase *hakuna matata,* and they tell him it means "no worries." This translation though, is not a word for word but thought for thought.

This phrase is in Swahili, and sometimes Lingala and Swahili have overlapping words. Let's take *hakuna* for instances. In Lingala, the word *kuna* means "over there" or "there". In Swahili, it still encompasses this concept with a slight twist. Word for word *hakuna* means "there is, not here." *Matata* means the same in both Lingala and Swahili: trouble or problems.

In English then, the word for word meaning would be "trouble is over there not here" while the thought for thought translation would be "no worries." In this same way, when someone is using the gift of interpretation, they are not going to always interpret word for word. They may just get the thought and articulate it.

In the Old Testament, Daniel was a great example of someone interpreting tongues. In Daniel 5, we find the story of King Nebuchadnezzar's son, Belshazzar. Belshazzar threw a party and invited a thousand of his lords. During the party, he decided to go get the vessels that his father took from the temple of the God of Israel and use them to drink with.

Right after he starts using the vessels, a finger appears and writes words on the wall. The king is stricken with fear and says, "Whoever reads this writing, and shows me its interpretation, shall be clothed with purple and have a chain of gold around his neck and shall be the third ruler in the kingdom" (Daniel 5:7).

After this statement the queen enters the banquet because of the commotion and tells the king about Daniel. The King calls Daniel, and he interprets the heavenly language. The words written on the wall were *mene, mene, tekel* and *parsin* (Daniel 5:25).

Daniel then gave this interpretation:

"Mene, God has numbered the days of your kingdom and brought it to an end; Tekel, you have been weighed in the balances and found wanting; Peres, your kingdom is divided and given to the Medes and Persians" (Daniel 5:26-28).

Notice how this was not a word for word translation, but what each word's definition encompassed. This is how interpretations of tongues work. It doesn't mean one can't interpret word for word, but that each interpretation can vary based on the leading of the Holy Spirit.

But there are other things **we can also learn from Daniel as it relates to interpretation. One, he never forces it.** In Daniel 2, King Nebuchadnezzar has a dream and demands the wise man, the enchanters, and magicians of Babylon to tell him first what his own dream is and then tells them to interpret it. If they can't, he threatens to kill them. When Daniel discovers this, he asks the king for time. He notifies his friends, and they all pray until God reveals the dream and interpretation.

Secondly, Daniel never takes credit for interpreting the dream, but gives all the glory to God. Right after he receives the interpretation, he gives God glory (Daniel 2:20-23). Then, when King Nebuchadnezzar asks him, *"'Are you able to make known to me the dream that I have seen and its interpretation?" Daniel responds by saying, "'No wise men, enchanters, magicians, or astrologers can show to the king the mystery that the king has asked, but there is a God in heaven who reveals mysteries (Daniel 2:26-28).'"* **Daniel never tried to usurp the glory of God; he instead, deflected all praise that came towards him right back to God.**

Lastly, an individual should never allow financial gain to be the goal of using their gifts. In Daniel 5, he didn't interpret the heavenly language for the king in order to receive gifts. As a matter of fact, Daniel told the king to keep his gifts. The king pretty much had to force Daniel to take his offer. It was obvious that Daniel was not living to gain the temporal but was living for what is eternal.

As ministers, financial gain can be very enticing. If we're not careful, greed can fill our hearts as it did Elisha's servant Gehazi. In this story, Naaman the Syrian has leprosy and he seeks out healing for his leprosy in Israel.

Elisha invites him and instructs him to wash himself in the Jordan seven times. After complaining about going in the Jordan River, Naaman concedes and gets healed. He is so overwhelmed after his healing that he tries to pay Elisha for healing him.

Elisha turns down the money and instructs him to go in peace. However, Elisha's servant Gehazi chases Naaman down and takes the money. When Gehazi comes back from taking money from Naaman, Elisha confronts him.

"Elisha said, *'Where have you been, Gehazi?' And he said, 'Your servant went nowhere.' But he said to him, 'Did not my heart go when the man turned from his chariot to meet you? Was it a time to accept money and garments, olive orchards and vineyards, sheep and oxen, male servants and female servants? Therefore, the leprosy of Naaman shall cling to you and to your descendants forever.' So he went out from his presence a leper, like snow"* (2 Kings 5:25-27).

The core of the message is this: Naaman's story depicts the grace of God, and Jesus uses his story to explain the Gospel to the Pharisees.

He says that *"there were many lepers in Israel in the time of the prophet Elisha, and none of them was cleansed, but only Naaman the Syrian"* (Luke 4:27). What Elisha was doing in the Old Testament had more ramifications than just a leper being healed. When he states to Gehazi, "*Was it a time to accept money and garments, olive orchards and vineyards, sheep and oxen, male servants and female servants?" (2 Kings 5:27)* **I believe he says this because Naaman's healing should reflect the grace of God, and God's grace cannot be bought.** Naaman says,

"If not, please let there be given to your servant two mule loads of earth, for from now on your servant will not offer burnt offering or sacrifice to any god but the Lord. In this matter may the Lord pardon your servant: when my master goes into the house of Rimmon to worship there, leaning on my arm, and I bow myself in the house of Rimmon, when I bow myself in the house of Rimmon, the Lord pardon your servant in this matter" (2 Kings 5:17-18).

Elisha responds by saying, *"Go in peace" (2 Kings 5:19).* **Elisha did not take the time to address Naaman's actions because the gospel is less concerned with a person's outward presentation and more about how a person positions their heart.** We as ministers can learn a lot from this story. In no way am I saying ministers should not be paid. The Bible says, *"You shall not muzzle an ox when it treads out the grain,"* and *"The laborer deserves his wages" (1 Timothy 5:18).* Solomon even writes, *"Wisdom is even better when you have money. Both are a benefit as you go through life" (Ecclesiastes 7:11 NLT).*

The gospel should always take precedence in every situation. This means there may be times where God asks you to turn down a large sum of money for the sake of advancing His kingdom. If your heart in these moments is not positioned right, you could act in such a way where you would end up reaping destruction. Like Daniel and Elisha, we must never use our gifts for selfish gain.

CHAPTER 24

Prophecy

Many churches today don't believe that God still speaks through people. If someone were to say they had a prophetic word from the Lord, that person may risk being kicked out. In other churches, a prophetic word may be accepted as secondary to the church's prevailing views. It seems that only *some* churches honor a prophetic word given by a man or woman of God.

According to Paul, we should *"pursue love, and earnestly desire the spiritual gifts, especially that you may prophesy" (1 Corinthians 14:1). Earnestly desire* can be translated to mean "covet earnestly" (KJV). **In other words, we must desperately take pleasure in, or lust after, the spiritual gifts, and "especially that [we] may prophecy."** So why don't we long for the gifts in this fashion?

Like most things in life, people forsake what they don't understand and slowly embrace what's explained. Considering this let's look at what the spiritual gift of prophecy is and how we are to use it.

As established earlier in the personality gifts, the word prophecy is diverse. **There is forthtelling, which is declaring the truth of God's word to people, and then there is foretelling, which is proclaiming future events before they occur based on the word of God being the source of the proclamation.** This concept of proclaiming future events is based on the truth that the Spirit of God declares to us things that are to come (John 16:13).

To better understand prophecy, we must look at the prophetic word and how people responded to it in Scripture. Acts 21:10-14 is a great place to start to accurately understand the nuances of prophecy. During this time, Paul went to Caesarea and met with Philip the Evangelist, who happened to have four daughters who prophesied. After meeting with Philip, a prophet by the name of Agabus came to Paul.

"And coming to us, he took Paul's belt and bound his own feet and hands and said, 'Thus says the Holy Spirit, 'This is how the Jews at Jerusalem will bind the man who owns this belt and deliver him into the hands of the Gentiles'"" (Acts 21:11).

There are several things we can learn from this prophetic word. **One, prophecy can seem weird.** We read that Agabus, "took Paul's belt and bound his own feet and hands." This would be very strange, yet it happened. Some people get turned off by the prophetic because they believe it's weird, but in the Bible, many foolish things look wise and wise things look foolish (1 Corinthians 1:27).

Notice what he says before he speaks: "Thus says the Holy Spirit…". Apparently, God still speaks to us and through us. This does not mean every prophetic word should start this way, but it still speaks to the foundation of prophecy. It's not the man who comes up with the prophetic word but God who moves on man.

It then goes on to say, *"'This is how the Jews at Jerusalem will bind the man who owns this belt and deliver him into the hands of the Gentiles.'"* The prophecy was not about Paul's past but his future, thus forthtelling. It was a warning.

Now Paul, being a mature Christian, heard the words given to him but did not allow these words to deter God's plan. He knew he was going to suffer for Christ, so this was a confirmation for him. He responded, *"What are you doing, weeping and breaking my heart? For I am ready not only to be imprisoned but even to die in Jerusalem for the name of the Lord Jesus"* (Acts 21:13).

Paul did not call him a false prophet because what he said did not make him "feel better." They persisted to warn Paul until they realized he was not going to change his course because God was controlling it. At this point, they all said, "let the will of God be done." **Giving a prophetic word does not mean receiving your intended outcome, because just like the words are from God, the outcome also is in his hands.**

We know that Prophet Agabus' word he gave came true. Paul was arrested and bound and killed for the gospel. This passage always amazes me because when you think about it if this was to happen today, people would place blame.

People would say statements like "the word was given wrong" or "the person responding was too proud." But when we truly examine the Word of God we begin to see. **Prophecy indicates, but does not always dictate, a person's choice.**

So how should we respond to prophecy? The first thing we need to do is have a proper attitude toward it. 1 Thessalonians 5:20 states that we are not to despise prophecy. The implication of this verse is at times overlooked. Significantly Paul is using the antithesis of importance to elevate prophecy.

Secondly, we are supposed to test every spirit (1 Thessalonians 5:21). How do we test prophecy? First, it must line up with the Word of God. 2 Timothy 3:16-17 states that *"All Scripture is breathed out by God and profitable for teaching, for reproof, for correction, and for training in righteousness, that the man of God may be complete, equipped for every good work."* **Since God's word reflects Him, if you receive a prophetic word that does not line up with His Word, it's not from Him.**

Next, there must be a confirmation in your spirit. In essence, God will most likely have been speaking to your heart already. **I say "most likely" because there are times when our disobedience closes our ears from hearing the truth, and in our defiance, it's the voice of God that we've silenced.**

Third, one must discern what manner of spirit someone is using. Satan brought what seemed like a prophetic word to Jesus. While tempting him, he told Jesus

"If you are the Son of God, throw yourself down, for it is written, 'He will command his angels concerning you,' and 'On their hands they will bear you up, lest you strike your foot against a stone'" (Matthew 4:6).

There are several truths here. Jesus was the Son of God, and in Psalm 91, it is written that God would send his angels to protect us. However, Scripture interprets Scripture. God will not contradict Himself, and therefore Jesus' responded by saying, *"It is also written 'You shall not put the Lord your God to the test'" (Matthew 4:7).*

Lastly, prophecy should be a spiritual weapon. Paul puts this way:

"This charge I entrust to you, Timothy, my child, in accordance with the prophecies previously made about you, that by them you may wage the good warfare, holding faith and a good conscience. By rejecting this, some have made shipwreck of their

faith, among whom are Hymenaeus and Alexander, whom I have handed over to

Satan that they may learn not to blaspheme" (1 Timothy 1:18-20).

He tells Timothy that by the prophetic words that were spoken over his life he should wage a "good warfare." The substance of this statement is this: let's say you've been praying for a house, and someone gives you a prophetic word and says, "God is showing me a new house." When you hear this, you should write it down and make it a prayer emphasis because every prophecy invites a level of conflict.

The devil and his minions may have heard the word too, and through discouragement or wrong timing, they may try to veer you off the right path. As you are praying and keeping the matter before God, you are warring in the spirit. Now anytime discouragement comes, you will not be moved because you are aware of what the Lord spoke. Fear will not cause you to stray from God's promises because you know what He has declared over you.

In the last part of these verses Paul has some very harsh words for some people whom he names by name that had neglected prophecy and holding faith to a good conscience. In 1 Timothy 1:18-20, he says: *"By rejecting this, some have made shipwreck of their faith, among whom are Hymenaeus and Alexander, whom I have handed over to Satan that they may learn not to blaspheme."* By rejecting *what*? If one follows the flow of thought, it is indeed indicating that by rejecting the prophetic word and not holding faith and a good conscience, some of them had shipwrecked their faith. Their lives got so bad that Paul said he had to hand them over to Satan, a statement he first made in 1 Corinthians 5 to refer to an individual who willfully sins and refuses to repent. If Paul had such harsh words to say about those who neglected prophecy,

shouldn't we put more magnitude on receiving and responding to prophecy?

CHAPTER 25

The Knowing Gifts: Word of Knowledge

Word of knowledge is not to be mistaken with worldly knowledge. Worldly knowledge is gained from books; word of knowledge is given by the Holy Spirit. Knowledge in the world leads people to always be learning but never coming to the knowledge of truth (2 Timothy 3:7). This is usually because truth is a partial goal but looking or being intelligible is the other part of the goal. A true word of knowledge works from knowing truth and revealing truth, while worldly knowledge starts from not knowing the truth and hoping to discover truth that suits the pursuer.

The three gifts that I believe can sometimes be mistaken for each other are the gifts of prophecy, godly wisdom, and the word of knowledge. Each are normally used to help guide people by giving them unique information about life's circumstantial situations.

Take godly wisdom, for instance. When a person is giving wise advice, it can sound prophetic. *"Train up a child in the way he should go; even when he is old he will not depart from it" (Proverbs 22:6).* Does this mean every person that is trained as a child doesn't ever stray from this training when they get older? Or is it saying it's harder for a child to stray from what they've learned earlier on in life?

Word of knowledge is mistaken for prophecy not because they sound the same, but because they can be presented the same. But there is a way to truly differentiate between the two, and it has to do with past, present, and future. **Word of knowledge is**

a supernatural knowing of something that is in the past or that adheres to a person's present situation.

One of the best examples of the word of knowledge is from the Old Testament, after David fell into sin with Bathsheba. The story is found in 2 Samuel 11:1-24; 12:1-23. David committed adultery and attempted to cover it up by murdering the husband of the woman he slept with. He thought it was all hidden, but God knows everything.

A prophet by the name of Nathan came one day into the throne room of David and told him a story about a man who had plenty of sheep but chose to steal a poor man's only sheep. Telling the story by Nathan was a wise way to confront David. David was angry to hear that someone would do such a thing and Nathan told him he, David, was that man.

This was a word of knowledge in action. Nathan knew about David's past without David having told him. **He used this gift not to boast, make money, or beat David down. He used it to glorify God and to get David to see his fault in hopes he would repent, which he did.**

After the word of knowledge, Nathan then said this to David:

"Thus says the Lord, 'Behold, I will raise up evil against you out of your own house. And I will take your wives before your eyes and give them to your neighbor, and he shall lie with your wives in the sight of this sun. For you did it secretly, but I will do this thing before all Israel and before the sun.' David said to Nathan, 'I have sinned against the Lord.' And Nathan said to David, 'The Lord also has put away your sin;

you shall not die. Nevertheless, because by this deed you have utterly scorned the Lord, the child who is born to you shall die.'" (2 Samuel 12:11-14)

This now is a prophetic word that is given to David and it is without condition. In other words, it will happen whether David prays or not. The first part of this prophecy happens in 2 Samuel 16:22, when David's son Absalom sleeps with his father's concubines in public. The latter part of the prophetic word happens right away in the following verses after Nathan departs. **David's son dies and the implication of the innocent dying for the guilty is indeed foreshadowing of Christ's death for us.**

Any gift used in a wrong way can be detrimental. However, Word of Knowledge is by far more damaging because you can't judge the heart by the gift. For instance, I've known people who were doing witchcraft and yet were completely "accurate" about what had happened or was currently happening in an individual's life.

Predicting the future is hard for the enemy because he is a created being who has an end, but God was and is and will be. When it comes to past situations, though, the devil can display some deceptive knowledge.

First, he is a spiritual being, which means his communication is not just at our fleshly level. He can also communicate with our spirit and soul. Mix this with the fact that he has his demonic agents influencing our lives on a daily basis, and this is how you end up with psychics. These are people who through the manipulation of the demonic realm gather information from spiritual informants, who are the cause agents of many of the situations in the first place.

Today there's a whole movement of "good" mediums who will tell you about your past and present situation, and if you're under their influence, they will dictate your future and pretend to prophecy as if the demons did not fabricate the entire thing themselves. But going down this route will cost you something, and the further you go the more you owe until what you pay is your soul.

These people who manipulate the word of knowledge can be known by their fruit that does not mature. There are two ways to examine individuals using the gifts. First and foremost, their relationship with Jesus only. By saying "Jesus only," I'm in no way neglecting the trinity but acknowledging that it is *"in Christ all the fullness of the Deity lives in bodily form, and in Christ you have been brought to fullness. He is the head over every power and authority" (Colossians 2:9-10).* If they say Jesus plus anything else other than the triune God, run the other way.

Secondly, you can look at the fruits of the Spirit (Galatians 5:22-23). If these fruits are not in them, then Christ is not in them. When someone is prideful in their gifting, it doesn't matter how amazing their gifting is. Jesus showed us how we are to present the gospel by dying for us, serving us, and elevating us. Furthermore, as written previously, if their fruit never matures after years of serving God, the seed has not truly been wholeheartedly implemented in their hearts. **Now there is difference in immaturity that is warranted and immaturity that is gratuitous, and I want to illustrate this through my own personal encounter with spiritual gifts.**

When I first arrived to SAGU, I had no idea how to truly use the gifts. I remember one time I passed one of my friends while I was walking, and I sensed something in my spirit about her. I felt as if she had a crush on one of my other friends. Being young and lacking knowledge, I turned around quickly and asked my friend "Do you like so and so?" She was so shocked by this gesture that she immediately shouted no! But then, realizing she lied to me, she said "Yes, how did you know that?"

In my mind, I immediately concluded that there was no way I could have possibly just guessed that, so the information must have come from God. If it did come from God, this meant that my friend and my other friend were meant to be together. On top of this, I had a huge inclination that no one was going to love my friend like this woman was going to. So, I went to my other friend and told him, "I think I may know who your wife is." I shared with him also how I felt like no one was going to love him like this woman was going to.

My friend, longing to please God and knowing that I had received accurate words from God before, said, "Brother I do not feel the same way about her, but I will pray about it." After intently praying about it he came back and told me that he had no peace. I was devastated. I thought to myself, *why would God allow me to know information only to lead people astray?* Bewildered and confused, I pulled away from sharing what I felt in fear of leading more people the wrong way.

It took me years to realize my mistake, and it's a mistake many Christians make when they operate in their gifts. Like anything else we must mature in our giftings and have room to mature. The seriousness of getting a prophetic word wrong is not to be overlooked, in the same token, the seriousness of not being too shy to give a word that God places on your heart should not be overlooked either. Both can be detrimental, so we must not be quick to silence the gifts just because they are abused or misused. On the other hand, we must be willing to be taught by humbly, admitting when we are wrong.

What I did wrong was I assumed that since I knew part of something, it meant I could see the unknown. However, knowing something doesn't mean you know *everything* about that one thing. Word of knowledge has to do with past and present. You can say through word of knowledge that the past becomes a present. So just because I may have sensed that my friend had feelings for my other friend, it didn't mean I could see into their future. Maybe God just wanted me to pray for my friend who was dealing with all these emotions.

When we don't ask the Holy Spirit further questions about the information, we may acquire through the giftings, then we are like people who may need glasses and refuse to put them on while driving. Since our vision is impaired, we can crash.

CHAPTER 26

The Knowing Gifts: Word of Wisdom

When one speaks about word of wisdom, it's important to clarify the difference between worldly wisdom, godly wisdom, and a word of wisdom. In the book of James, we get a pretty good definition of what worldly wisdom and godly wisdom are.

In describing worldly wisdom, James states,

"But if you have bitter jealousy and selfish ambition in your hearts, do not boast and be false to the truth. This is not the wisdom that comes down from above, but is earthly, unspiritual, demonic. For where jealousy and selfish ambition exist, there will be disorder and every vile practice" (James 3:14-16).

According to James, wisdom that's not from God is earthly, unspiritual, and demonic. And how a person can recognize this type of wisdom is that the fruit of it is bitter jealousy and selfish ambition in the heart.

The fruits of this type of wisdom create an environment filled with disorder and evil practices. For instance, the wise people of this world believe that homosexuality is a natural way of life, yet the Bible calls it an evil practice. Jealousy and selfish ambition literally give birth to murder, rape, perversion, stealing, hate, and sexual immorality.

James goes on to say,

"But the wisdom from above is first pure, then peaceable, gentle, open to reason, full of mercy and good fruits, impartial and sincere. And a harvest of righteousness is sown in peace by those who make peace" (James 3:17-18).

There are eight things that make up godly wisdom. These eight things are purity, a peaceable spirit, gentle, open to reason, full of mercy, good fruits, impartial, and sincere. Each one of these attributes is important if we want to walk in wisdom from above.

How often do we hear people say something wise and we immediately jump to the conclusion that the person must be wise? As we have just read from James, character helps us identify what wisdom looks like. Therefore, I believe godly wisdom is often grown through trials of various kinds. Now, someone can be used by the spirit of God to give a word of wisdom and not truly be wise. Or, someone can say what may seem like a wise principle, and when this principle is examined through the lens of what the Holy Spirit is saying, the statement may turn out to be demonically inspired and selfish in nature.

A great example of a person who made what seemed to many like a wise statement is found in the Gospel of John. John writes about a time when Jesus came to Bethany right after he raised Lazarus from the dead.

While at Bethany, Jesus was invited to eat. He was sitting down, reclined on the ground, when Mary came in and anointed his feet and washed it with her hair. Immediately Judas, one of the disciples, spoke up and said, *"Why was this ointment not sold for three hundred denarii and given to the poor?" (John 12:5)*

If you look at this statement from the perspective of the other gospels (Matthew 26:6-13, Luke 7:36-50, and Mark 14:3-9), you can get a better understanding of Judas' statement. In hindsight, we know that Judas was actually a greedy thief, which is why he made this statement to begin with. But there is no indication from the Word of God that can lead us to conclude that all of the disciples knew he was a thief.

On the contrary, the position in the group that Judas had as financial overseer could lead one to see him as someone who was trusted by the others. So, when he made the statement about selling the ointment and giving the money to the poor, the disciples and others who were in the room did not dismiss him but agreed with him.

Why did they agree with him? Well, in the book of Proverbs there are many "truisms" about people giving to the poor. Thus, why those in the room did not see anything wrong with his statement, allowing Judas to masquerade his motives. Yet Jesus' response was in direct contrast to Judas' statement, helping to expose Judas' hidden worldly wisdom.

Jesus responded by saying, *"Leave her alone, so that she may keep it for the day of my burial. For the poor you always have with you, but you do not always have me."* In connection to what Jesus said is the truth that true wisdom is staying in step with what the Holy Spirit is doing and saying, even if it may seem foolish now. Therefore Paul writes in 1 Corinthians 1:18-31 and chapter 2 about how godly wisdom is seen as folly to the world.

In continuation, this is the difference between godly wisdom and a word of wisdom. Although both are from God, one is an overflow of the Holy Spirit operating in you. The word of wisdom has to do with an overflow of the Holy Spirit indwelling in you. The best example would be circumstantial.

This is what I mean: **anyone can pray for wisdom from God, as James states that He gives it without reproach. When this type of wisdom manifests, it is action prone; one has to walk and apply what has been invested inside.** The word of wisdom, on the other hand, is used when different circumstances arise as if one has already faced the circumstantial situations before. **The word of wisdom refers to being influenced by the Spirit to alter human perspective by aligning with the will of God as the occasion arises. It is making the right judgement on a matter and getting insight when it matters.**

One can be used in your personal walk with God while the other is simply for the body to be edified. Regarding the wisdom gained from praying, as James says, anyone can ask for it and any one can gain it. Sometimes though, it's birthed through trials, either yours or listening to someone else's life experiences. This type of wisdom is more of a personal attribute that edifies you while the word of wisdom is for the body's edification, and although the Holy Spirit may use anyone, there are specific people who flow more naturally in it.

All in all, *"If you are wise, you are wise for yourself; if you scoff, you alone will bear it" (Proverbs 9:12).* **Being wise helps you first while the word of wisdom helps others first.**

CHAPTER 27

The Knowing Gifts: Discernment of Spirits

During my time at SAGU, I was nominated to be over all the on-campus ministries, one of which was prayer. I was young, naive, and full of zeal. I rounded up some leaders after I prayed, and we started having prayer meetings once a week. During this time, we heard a story about a pastor who was in a city that had one of the highest murder rates in the world. Sick of the evil, he decided to gather some churches and pray nonstop the whole weekend. That weekend, not one person died.

This story inspired us, and we thought if this happened for him, it could surely happen for us. We decided to initiate all-night prayers. One Friday a month, we would pray from 11 pm-6 am because we wanted God to move in our school and change our nation. There were only about ten of us at first, but we didn't care. We were hungry for God.

As time went on, more college kids heard about the meetings and all that God had been doing and they started coming. One Friday night we had 50 people stay the whole night, just crying out to God. The following month, when it came time for the next all-night prayer each one of the leaders felt in their heart like something unique was going to happen but could not pinpoint exactly what it was going to be.

Normally, the leaders would all meet an hour before the all-night prayer to pray for the event and discuss anything we felt God was saying. This specific day, people were busy and when we did meet, the meeting was disorganized. Instead of discussing and praying about all-night prayer, some of us in the group were telling stories about all sorts of stuff. By the time we started talking about the all-night prayer we only had ten minutes left, and because of this, we did not discern what the Holy Spirit was saying. As we walked out of the office to all-night prayer, there was a crowd of people in the prayer room larger than we had ever seen.

The room could only hold 75 people, and 80+ people showed up. We weren't even able to close the door, so many people had to stay in the foyer. The worship leader started praising God on the keyboard, and immediately the presence of God filled the room. Everyone started worshipping, and when I looked around the room, everyone's hands were up in the air. It was a beautiful sight to behold.

Not too long after we began worshipping, a man came up to me and another one of my leaders. As he approached us, he had a concerned face. He told us there was a man who was from India in the room who had been demonically possessed for years and no one could cast the demons out of him. My leader and I approached the man, who looked completely distraught. **This is where we started making a series of mistakes.**

First, we did not truly discern what was causing this manifestation. We brought the man to the middle of the room and told everyone that we were going to cast the demon out of this man. After he was in the middle of the room everyone started praying corporately, but it was not in unity. Some were screaming "demon, leave!" others "demon, be bound!" while others were saying "demon, be set on fire."

Every time we all would pray; the man would make a face as if he was constipated. Then he would throw his head back, slide his top lip to the left and bottom lip to the right, and scream "RACA!!!!" **In my heart I saw the word lie, but I didn't take**

the time to discern why the Holy Spirit had spoken that word in my heart. We finally realized that everyone screaming at the top of their lungs was not going to work, so we sent everyone into the foyer except the leaders. We now had put Jesus on the back burner and gave the devil center stage.

All the students went out and the leaders stayed inside the prayer room while one of the leaders and I dealt with the demon possessed man. The other leaders were interceding around us, but Jean and I still felt stuck. Every time we would tell the demonic spirit to leave, the man would throw his head back, put on his constipated face, shift his lips, and scream "RACA!!!!" Jean and I searched through the Word of God in hopes that we could find a solution.

We knew there was a place in the Bible where Jesus said that if you called someone raca, which meant "fool", you were deserving of hell fire (Matthew 5:22). Was this man calling us fools? Was he acting foolishly? Was this a spirit of foolishness? As we wrestled with these thoughts someone came and tapped me on the shoulder. I turned around I saw that it was a student we had sent out. His eyes were full of tears as he said to me, "I'm not demon possessed." I looked at his eyes and I said, "you're not demon possessed", and I prayed for him.

Strange, I thought to myself. As I turned around, another person came and tapped my shoulder. "There's a kid manifesting demons out there," he said. When I investigated the foyer, I saw one of my friends moving as if he was gliding on the ground. He glided his way all the way to where I was and just stood there with his eyes rolled back, moving like an avatar from a street fighter game when no one is pushing a button on the controller. I immediately screamed "Fire!!!" And my friend fell to the

146

ground under the power of the Holy Spirit. When he stood up, he looked at me with a perturbed face and said, "What happened?"

After explaining to him what took place, he said he could not remember how he got in the room. I turned and looked at the man saying "Raca" and was puzzled. How could I cast a demon out of one person but not another? One by one people started coming in and tapping me on the shoulder and asking me if I thought they were demon possessed. *What in the world is going on?* I thought. Finally, I called everyone into the room. I had to straighten this out.

Little did I know what had transpired in the foyer. **Apparently, while the leaders were inside with the man saying "Raca", there was another person outside wreaking havoc.** According to one of the witnesses and others who were in the foyer, there was a man who was going to individuals and telling them that they were demon possessed and that they needed to go to me to pray for them. He also went to my friend Andre and screamed, "GOD CAN'T HEAR YOU, PRAY LOUDER!!" My friend panicked and wrapped both of his arms around his Bible tightly and crouched down.

Many of the students were so terrified that they ran back to their dorms. After this, I told everyone to come back in only about 60 people came in. Everyone was in an uproar. One of my leaders stood up on a bench and pointed at a person who was holding the mic and said, "You have the spirit of lust!" and the individual said humbly "Yes, I know I do."

While all this commotion was going on, the individual who was outside with everyone was still going to people behind my back and telling them, "You're demon possessed, go to Gloire so he can pray for you." People started tapping me on the back fearfully, asking if they were demon possessed. This whole time we could not discern what was going on. We knew there was confusion, but we did not know the cause.

Eventually God had grace on us. The man who was telling people they were demon possessed made a huge mistake. He went to Jean and said to him, "You're demon possessed." Jean turned around quickly and loudly responded, "I KNOW I'M NOT DEMON POSSESSED; YOU'RE DEMON POSSESSED!!!"

When I heard him, I turned toward the man and I felt righteous indignation flowing through my veins. My leaders gathered behind me and the man started walking backwards. The demons in him were begging me not to cast them out. As I walked towards him, he had his hands out front and the spirits in him were saying, "Gloire! No! Please don't!"

As he moved backwards people split from either side like the Red Sea. Frustrated and righteously indignant I screamed, "FIRE!!" and the man fell down on the ground and the demons left him. **After that, the rest of the night went amazing, and God worked many wonders.**

The following week after the all-night prayer, I went to see the professor who was over me. I knew I was going to be in trouble, because word about the crazy prayer meeting had spread. I hoped he would at least hear me out. When I came in, he was not happy. He asked me what had happened, and I proceeded to tell him that we should have been more prepared and that the devil came after us.

After listening, he thought it best to cancel prayer.

Cancel prayer? I couldn't believe what I heard. I left the room so depressed. I went downstairs to chapel, frustrated and depressed. At this time, I ran into the president of the campus and he looked at me and said, "Why so down Gloire?" I responded, "Prayer is canceled."

He looked at me with such a shock on his face. Then he said, "I heard about what happened last night. I believe the devil attacked you guys and I think there should be a teacher who stays all night with y'all. If you can't find one, I'm willing to stay up all night." I was amazed and immediately relieved!

Apparently, one of my leaders had discerned the situation and sent an email to the president right after the prayer meeting. By the grace of God, he had already heard about it before any of the complaints came in. He discerned what was said rightly and judged the situation rightly.

I tell this story to place great emphasis on discernment. We were all discerning something, but we did not know the source of what we were discerning. Our discernment was immature; it was more of an intuition. When one gets a hunch about something but does not know what spirit is behind that hunch, it's more intuitive than discerning. **Discerning maturely has to do with knowing what spirit is manifesting and influencing an individual or situation.**

Reflecting on the situation, there are a few things we should have done. One, we should have prayed together longer until we truly understood what it was, we were sensing. We also should have never given the devil center stage. The devil is always trying to find a way to steal glory from God. When we put the man, who was saying "Raca" in the middle we went from seeking God to showcasing our power of God. **It became more about what we know instead of what He knows.** This does not mean deliverance is not necessary, because it is, but it must be done in an orderly fashion.

In connection to this is the word "lie" I saw in my heart. **The Holy Spirit I believe was trying to get my attention, I just did not know Him well enough to clearly understand.** Honestly, I think that the man who was saying "Raca" was dealing with a lie the enemy had caused him to believe. At the same time, the devil was lying to us because he wanted to cause confusion in the room.

I should have never sent everyone out and left the leaders inside. We all should have kept our focus on God and two leaders could have taken the man out and dealt with him privately.

Lastly, we should have asked God for discernment. It's taken me awhile, but I've finally realized that even though discernment isn't my initial gift it does not mean I can't operate in it if the issue arises. We can still ask the Holy Spirit to help us discern situations and people's motives. We have not because we ask not, and we receive not because we ask selfishly (James 2). We can all grow and learn how to be more discerning of people and situations if we ask God, humble ourselves, and learn from those who do readily flow in the gift of discernment.

I believe the leader who sent the email to the president flowed in the gift of discernment. Yet even her gift had to grow. There were times during that night where she became suspicious of some people in the room. When she called out the individual struggling with lust, she was correct about what she discerned; however, she did it in a way that embarrassed the person.

When discernment is in the flesh, it can become an evil suspicion (1 Timothy 6:4). In the Bible, after David became king, he heard that his friend Nashan the King of Amon passed away and his son, Hanun, was now reigning in his place.

Since David had a great relationship with Nashan, he thought he would show the same kindness to his son.

David sent an envoy through some of his men to Hanun stating his desire to show kindness towards him because of his father's death. **But Hanun gave into the evil suspicion of his princes**.

"...The princes of the Ammonites said to Hanun, "Do you think, because David has sent comforters to you, that he is honoring your father? Have not his servants come to you to search and to overthrow and to spy out the land?" (1 Chronicles 19:3)

Without evidence, the evil suspicion led Hanun and he *"...took David's servants and shaved them and cut off their garments in the middle, at their hips, and sent them away." (1 Chronicles 19:4)*

This brought great shame to David's men. Instead of realizing that he was wrong, however, Hanun reached out to other kingdoms and got them involved. They went after David to destroy him, but the Lord was with David, and he overcame all of them.

We can learn so much from this situation. An evil suspicion started a war. When people are suspicious of others, it destroys relationships and causes them to gang up on others without reason. In so doing we will eventually be destroyed by our actions if we do not repent because one of the six things God hates is someone who bears a false witness and sows' discord (Proverbs 6:16-19).

Discernment does not aim to fight the man but the spirit behind the evil actions of an individual. Evil suspicion views a man who knows the Lord as the source of evil. One who discerns a situation will not slander an individual to prove their point while one who suspects a person of evil will perpetuate their beliefs to everyone to prove themselves right and make the one, they deem as the suspect feel guilty. Discernment seeks repentance and evil suspicion seeks destruction.

CHAPTER 28

Deliverance and The Gift of Discernment

The word deliverance scares a lot of people in the church because there have been so many immature Christians who have abused deliverance. Some people would think that people have to roll around like a snake and foam at the mouth, but deliverance doesn't always look like this.

What is deliverance? In Luke, Jesus describes his ministry by quoting what Isaiah had written about Him. In the story we read about how Jesus would go up to the synagogue and read passages from the Old Testament. On this particular day, He opened Isaiah and read,

"The Spirit of the Lord is upon me,

because he has anointed me

to proclaim good news to the poor.

He has sent me to proclaim liberty to the captives

and recovering of sight to the blind,

to set at liberty those who are oppressed,

to proclaim the year of the Lord's favor." (Luke 4:18-19)

This is one of the best summaries of what Jesus came to do. Like Jesus, we also have been charged to carry this mantle. As the Spirit of the Lord was upon Jesus, it is also upon us. Therefore, we are charged to preach the good news as He did, proclaim freedom to the captives as He did, bring sight to the blind (take people out of spiritual prison) as He did, set at liberty those who are oppressed, bring deliverance, and proclaim the year of the Lord's favor the year of His salvation, as He did!

In churches today, however, we've become satisfied with programs. **So instead of walking in power we live programmed.** As a result, many in leadership are bound by lust, hate, jealousy, envy, selfish ambition, and sensuality, just to name a few things. But the worst part of it all is we don't believe that as believers, we can get demonized. Can a believer be demonized? Before we answer this question, let us look at what the Bible says.

Paul in many occasions addresses the influence Satan can have on believers. One place is found in Ephesians. Paul is in prison while writing this letter to the church in Ephesus, which is in what we know of as Turkey today.

Towards the end of the letter he states, *"'In your anger do not sin': Do not let the sun go down while you are still angry, and do not give the devil a foothold (Ephesians 4:26-27)."* The word "foothold" or "opportunity" in Greek is the word *topos*, which means "place." [1]

In other words, Paul is saying that if a believer lets the sun go down on their anger (in other words, does not forgive), then this person can give the devil a place in his life. Now the devil does not occupy space like we occupy space. I've heard it explained like this: **if the devil cannot be where believers are or dwell in the body of a believer because they have the presence of God, then the devil cannot be anywhere because God's presence is everywhere.**

I do not believe a demon can have *full control* of a believer; rather, I believe a believer can be oppressed by a demon and influenced by them. From what I've gathered from Scripture, demons can enter a believer's body and soul, but they cannot possess their spirit, since that is the throne room of the Holy Spirit.

A good example from the Bible is the lady with the crippled back. Luke, who is telling this story, is a physician, so when he speaks about Jesus healing, he is more detailed than the other writers.

"Now he was teaching in one of the synagogues on the Sabbath. And behold, there was a woman who had had a disabling spirit for eighteen years. She was bent over and could not fully straighten herself. When Jesus saw her, he called her over and said to her, 'Woman, you are freed from your disability.' And he laid his hands on her, and immediately she was made straight, and she glorified God. But the ruler of the synagogue, indignant because Jesus had healed on the Sabbath, said to the people, 'There are six days in which work ought to be done. Come on those days and be healed, and not on the Sabbath day.' Then the Lord answered him, 'You hypocrites! Does not each of you on the Sabbath untie his ox or his donkey from the manger and lead it away to water it? And ought not this woman, a daughter of Abraham whom Satan bound for eighteen years, be loosed from this bond on the Sabbath day?'" (Luke 13:10-16)

According to Luke, this was a spirit that had bound this lady for 18 years. Also, we know that she was someone who believed because Jesus called her a daughter of

Abraham (verse 16). The crippling spirit is what the Bible refers to as a spirit of infirmity. An infirmity (sickness or affliction) I believe is placed in a believer by a demonic entity. This can be cancer, various crippling ailments, headaches, depression, anxiety, addictions, many psychological issues, and many of the sicknesses we may face.

We are in a fight against the kingdom of darkness. Paul says,

"For we do not wrestle against flesh and blood, but against the rulers, against the authorities, against the cosmic powers over this present darkness, against the spiritual forces of evil in the heavenly places" (Ephesians 6:12).

Have you ever seen a wrestling match that was hands-off? Of course not. Paul purposely used the word *wrestling* because he knew we would be in hand to hand combat sometimes with the demonic. These demonic entities are not fleshly; they have spiritual bodies. It only makes sense that sometimes when we fight them it is our spiritual being engaging in this battle. They can bypass our flesh and torment our soul inside of us.

I've done deliverance with over 200 people who professed to know the Lord and have a relationship with Him, from pastors to children. Each had a different story but the same theme which was demonization. This is one of the reasons we need discernment of spirits.

My friend Jean and I once prayed for a Bible believing lady for three hours. While we were praying for her, she proudly looked at us as if we were fools. She would repeatedly say, "I'm a believer, there's nothing there."

However, when she we would speak, it was really fast, she would jump from one idea to another and it was not coherent. I'd almost feel like I was getting a headache just hearing her talk. But every time we prayed, nothing happened. She then went on to tell us how this minister she knew told her Christians cannot have demons.

I still felt though like there was something wrong. Jean and I prayed and finally Jean looked at me and said, "numbing spirit." She had a very nonchalant attitude. So, we asked if we could pray against the numbing spirit, and she reluctantly agreed. As we started to pray for her at first nothing was happening then all of a sudden, she screamed and then put her hand over her mouth. We then stopped and asked her what happened. She said, "sadness and depression left when I screamed."

She was a believer, so how did this happen? She gave the devil an opportunity somehow or the devil found an opportunity somehow and brought sadness into her life. Without the discernment of spirits, we would have never known what was hidden in this lady.

In no way am I saying that the demon's name was "numbing spirit". We just discerned what it was doing to her senses, which was causing her not to feel the presence of God nor be aware of the oppression in her life.

Without discernment, the church is unarmed. The devil will keep running rampant in our churches and many believers will remain bound. There is freedom in knowing! Pray for discernment!

Jesus once said, "But if it is by the finger of God that I cast out demons, then the Kingdom of God has come upon you" (Luke 11:20). Casting out devils is bringing the Kingdom of God!

CHAPTER 29

The Knowing Gifts and Dream Interpretation

My mother was the first person I encountered who interpreted dreams. She always would have very lively dreams. She would dream about war and instructions for life. I remember as I was growing up, I couldn't remember my dreams, and I assumed that I wasn't a dreamer.

One day, my mom asked me what I dreamed. I said, "I don't have dreams." "Yes, you do, you just can't remember them," she replied. She then went on to explain to me the importance of praying before you sleep and asking in prayer that God would speak to you in a dream. Also, she told me that sometimes the devil steals dreams or he causes your mind to forget the dreams you had that were too significant.
After hearing this, I went ahead and applied what my mom said and started to pray that I would remember my dream. I also prayed against the enemy stealing them or blinding me so that I couldn't remember. Sure enough, my dreams came back.

There has been much research done on dreams, and we are only scratching the surface. According to the National Sleep Foundation,

"You generally dream at least four to six times per night, usually during the most active REM stage of sleep if you're over 10 years old. (Kids younger than 10 dream only about 20 percent of the time in REM sleep.) You usually dream longer as the night goes on because the REM stage of sleep can be anywhere from five minutes early in the night to as long as 34 minutes towards the end of your sleep session. [1]

Even science agrees that everyone dreams. But why do we dream? I don't believe science can fully answer this question. The Bible, however, gives us insight about dreams. In Acts 2 after the disciples get baptized by the Holy Spirit with the evidence of speaking in tongues, Peter quotes Joel chapter 2 and says this about dreams:

"And in the last days it shall be, God declares, that I will pour out my Spirit on all flesh, and your sons and your daughters shall prophesy, and your young men shall see visions, and your old men shall dream dreams; even on my male servants and female servants in those days I will pour out my Spirit, and they shall prophesy"(Acts 2:17-18).

Peter clearly highlights that in the last days God will be communicating with us through dreams. I believe there are four main reasons why we dream: working out life's problems, random thoughts that some would call "pizza dreams", attacks from the devil, and most importantly, God communicating with us.

First, working out life's problems. Solomon said that, *"For a dream comes with much business, and a fool's voice with many words." (Ecclesiastes 5:3)* There have been many composers of music who have finished writing their music in their dreams.

Some mathematicians have solved equations likewise. So, the business of life can influence our dreams.

Next is the random dreams. These dreams I believe are random in that they don't really have meaning. One may be dreaming just because the brain never shuts down.

Then there are demonically inspired dreams that are sometimes called nightmares. Not every nightmare is from the devil because God will allow us to have dreadful dreams sometimes to draw us closer to him and away from sin. But bad sleep experiences, like sleep paralysis, come from the devil.

If you haven't heard of sleep paralysis, type the name in Google and look at the images people have drawn. They will shake you to the core. I've experienced them my whole life. They will normally start out as a dream that's like a horror movie. At every corner in the dream, you feel like something is going to jump out at you then eventually the climax of the dream is when that thing you felt jumps on you, and you can feel it physically.

I always know I'm having a demonic dream because it attacks my ability to speak. When I finally, with authority, say the name of Jesus, whatever was on me flees. The devil will also try to birth evil desires in your heart in dreams.

When I first got married, I would have dreams of me being with someone else other than my wife. The dreams would make it seem like I did not even know my wife when I would wake up my heart would physically hurt. I knew that the enemy was trying to put unfaithfulness in my heart so I would cheat on my wife.

Lastly, some dreams are God's way of communicating with us. **Dreams from God are given for a purpose.**

"For God speaks in one way, and in two, though man does not perceive it. In a dream, in a vision of the night, when deep sleep falls on men, while they slumber on their beds, then he opens the ears of men and terrifies them with warnings, that he may turn man aside from his deed and conceal pride from a man; he keeps back his soul from the pit, his life from perishing by the sword." (Job 33:14-18)

There are countless Scriptures in the Old Testament and New Testament where God is speaking to men through dreams (Genesis 20:3, Genesis 28:11-22, Genesis 40:8, Genesis 41:25-27, Numbers 12:6, Judges 7:13-15, 1 Kings 3:5, Daniel 7:1-3, Daniel 2, Matthew 1:20, Matthew 2:12, Matthew 2:13, Matthew 27:19).

Truly, it is important for believers to not negate their dreams because God could be speaking something vital for their life. But what do we do with the dreams we have? What I've observed from Scripture, and from my wife, is that God not only gives us dreams, but He also can give us their interpretation.

Throughout Scripture, it seems that every person God used to interpret dreams has similar traits: they are wise beyond their years and they operate in the knowing gifts.

Take Joseph for instance, who was sold into slavery at 17 by his own brothers. At each place he went, he was wise in how he dealt with the people and the things that were given to him. He feared God which led to an increase of knowledge in his life (Proverbs 1:7). He was eventually promoted after God gave him the interpretation to the dreams Pharaoh had (Genesis 37-50).

Solomon is another person whom God communicated with in a dream (1 Kings 3:1-15). He, too, was used highly in the knowing gifts. God showed up to Solomon in a dream and asked him, "What shall I give you?" Solomon did not ask for wealth, but an understanding mind to discern between right and wrong. This pleased God and so God gave him unmatched wisdom, discernment and knowledge (1 Kings 3:1-15; 2 Chronicles 1:11). Someone like Solomon, I believe, could be used readily to interpret dreams.

Then there's Daniel. After the children of Israel disobeyed God by not letting the land rest, He sent them off to exile in Babylon. While there, God raised up four Hebrew boys: Hananiah, Mishael, Azariah, and Daniel. The Bible says, *"As for these four youths, God gave them learning and skill in all literature and wisdom, and Daniel had understanding in all visions and dreams." (Daniel 1:17)*

Daniel was given understanding in all visions and dreams. I believe this was all connected to the wisdom God gave him. **It takes supernatural knowing to regularly discern purpose in a dream.**

Dream interpretation, I believe, is an extension of the knowing gifts. This doesn't mean God cannot use you to interpret dreams if you don't flow in the knowing gifts easily because He is God and He can choose to do as He wills. What I'm alluding to is from what I've observed from those who God either spoke to or interpreted dreams in Scripture. One common denominator was that God also gave them an understanding mind.

Now there are many "dream interpreters" out there full of all sorts of nonsensical ideas of what dreams mean. True dream interpretation stems from a genuine relationship with the Holy Spirit.

For instance, it is immature to assume that light in a dream always means something godly. We know that according to Scripture, even Satan masquerades himself as an angel of light (2 Corinthians 11:14). Therefore wisdom, discernment and knowledge are important as it relates to deciphering dreams.

Each gift can be manifested in your dreams because ultimately a dream from God is just God communicating His purpose with you. By each gift I mean you can have a dream where faith is represented, healing is taking place, prophecy is given, etc.

I had a friend who was longing to be baptized in the Holy Spirit. He came to me and my friends and for several hours we prayed with him and nothing happened. That night though he had a dream. In his dream he saw a pillar of fire falling from the sky towards the dorms. He was standing outside in the dream and he looked up and saw this fireball falling like it was going to hit him, so he took off running. As he was running, the fire hit the ground and suddenly, this unknown tongue started coming out of his mouth. It started as a dream and he woke up speaking in tongues in real life.

Understanding the gifts can help you better comprehend dreams. Praying for the knowing gifts can better help a person decipher the dreams. **Maturing in dream interpretation is allowing the Holy Spirit to be the interpreter.**

CHAPTER 30

The Power Gifts: Faith

In today's world people so readily use the word faith. Sometimes people say things like "have faith in me," or a coach may say "have faith in each other." But what is faith? How does one gain faith? And how do we apply it? To answer these questions, we need to comprehend the polarity between salvific faith and the gift of faith.

The topic of faith is not new. There have been countless men and women who have labored to bring clarity on this subject matter. One of the more popular explanations of salvific faith comes from the Protestant reformers in the 16th Century.

It was in the 15th century that Martin Luther brought about the Reformation to the Catholic Church. After his religious revolution, the movement continued long after his death. Many new doctrines were birthed during this time, one of which was the explanation of salvific faith.

There are three words that are used by many scholars to describe saving faith: *notitia*, *assensus*, and *fiducia*. These words are written in Latin and each definition reveals an aspect of salvation.

Notitia is defined as knowledge.[1] It speaks to the need for a true believer to know who Jesus is and that there is evidence of his death burial and resurrection. Notitia encompasses the mind of an individual; it is an intellectual belief.

Assensus is interpreted as belief agreement. The gospel must go beyond just an intellectual knowledge; one must believe in their heart that Jesus is real and the Bible is true, even if one may not see immediate evidence of what the Bible may say, If the Bible says it, it must be true.[2]

Fiducia simply can mean trust. This is also the meaning for the word faith in Greek-pistis, which means "persuasive trust." It's not just enough to know God is real or to believe He is who He says He is. One must trust that His plan for their life is the best plan.

The persuasion in faith, however, is not based on man's cunning or capabilities; rather on one's submission to God's abilities. A good example is found in Matthew 8, when the Roman centurion encounters Jesus. Jesus just finished ministering to the leper by laying hands on him and healing him.

As He continued His way, He entered a town called Capernaum, named after the prophet Nahum. As He enters this town a Roman centurion comes to Him and tells Jesus,

> *"'Lord, my servant is lying paralyzed at home, suffering terribly.' And he said to him, 'I will come and heal him.' But the centurion replied, 'Lord, I am not worthy to have you come under my roof, but only say the word, and my servant will be healed. For I too am a man under authority, with soldiers under me. And I say to one, 'Go,' and he goes, and to another, 'Come,' and he comes, and to my servant, 'Do this,' and he does it.' When Jesus heard this, he marveled and said to those who followed him, 'Truly, I tell you, with no one in Israel have I found such faith'" (Matthew 8:6-10).*

The Bible says that *"when Jesus heard this, he marveled and said to those who followed him, 'Truly, I tell you, with no one in Israel have I found such faith'"* (Matthew 8:10). What was it about this man's faith that caused Jesus to be so astonished? **It was his understanding of authority.**

The centurion was in fact saying Jesus you are Ruler, King, Lord and whatever you say I must put my trust in. In connection to the centurions' statement, faith should be linked to trust and obedience.

If you obey and trust God, you will act like Him. James puts it this way *"You believe that God is one; you do well. Even the demons believe—and shudder!" (James 2:19)* What separates our belief in Jesus from a demon's belief in Him is we obey and trust Jesus, and they do not. What demonstrates our obedience is when our faith is put to work by not just saying we're Christians, but actually walking and loving like Christ did.

Salvific faith, therefore, is faith that has to do with a person's mind, heart, and body submitted to an eternal God. This reminds me of how we are commanded to love God. *"You shall love the Lord your God with all your heart and with all your soul and with all your strength and with all your mind, and your neighbor as yourself" (Luke 10:27).* Saving faith declares one righteous; thus, the statement: *"...Abraham believed God, and it was counted to him as righteousness" (Romans 4:3).* **The gift of faith, however, does not make one righteous.**

Speaking to the church in Corinth, Paul says something about love that I believe expounds on the differentiation between salvific faith and the gift of faith. Paul said, *"And if I have prophetic powers, and understand all mysteries and all knowledge, and if I have all faith, so as to remove mountains, but have not love, I am nothing" (1*

Corinthians 13:2). **In other words, giftedness does not equate to godliness.**

With this established we can now truly decipher the gift of faith. The Hebrew writer says this about faith, *"Now faith is the substance of things hoped for, the evidence of things not seen" (Hebrews 11:1).* The word "hope" here is lost in translation. In the world we live in, people use hope to refer to wishful thinking.

What the writer means by hope here, though, is confidence. In other words, faith (persuasive trust) is the substance, namely of things already established by God from creation of old, presently not seen, waiting to manifest. We are confident in this truth that as the earth is grounded and fixed, God's promises are fixed and immovable. The "things" not seen in Hebrews 11:1 refers to that which has been eternally, that is present in the heavens, and prophetically written and proclaimed by God for the future.

The substance, confidence, and evidence all point to Christ. He is the source of our faith (Hebrews 12:2), and His words birth faith *"...faith comes from hearing, and hearing through the word of Christ" (Romans 10:17).* Faith is activated when one does what the Word says. *"But be doers of the word, and not hearers only, deceiving yourselves" (James 1:22).*

How does all this fit with the gift of faith? Before we go any further, I want to establish the fact that one does not need to have grandeur faith for God to respond. There are countless stories throughout Scripture of people who just heard of Jesus didn't know His words or ways but believed and received. The gift of faith, though, is not just for an individual to showcase their ability to trust God. It, like all the other gifts, is useful for spreading the gospel and encouraging others.

As previously mentioned, faith is persuasive trust. In connection to the gift of faith, this trust that persuades influences a person who has this gift in all they do. For them, it is impossible to see anything that is impossible for God, within His good nature, since in their eyes God has already given the answer before time and it's just waiting to manifest.

It is said that Peter did not walk on water but on the very word Jesus spoke, which was "come." Likewise, faith sees what to do and how to do it as the Word directs. In a dark world, the natural eyes cannot see the spiritual reality without the Word of God. David wrote, *"Your word is a lamp to my feet and a light to my path" (Psalms 119:105).*

After I got saved, the first passage I meditated on day and night was Psalm 23. Meditation is much more than just memorization. One can be mesmerized by what they memorized, but one imitates what they meditate. As I soaked in this Psalm its provoked faith in me to believe that God would meet all my needs.

Before I was saved, I played basketball religiously. I had dreams of going far in basketball. As Jesus came to my heart, all my aspirations to be in the NBA changed. I gave up my ability to have scholarships to D1 and D2 colleges and surrendered my will to God.

My youth pastor, Joel Sosa, had taken us to SAGU in Waxahachie Texas, when I was a junior in high school for a college visit. Upon arrival, I felt tremendous peace and I knew I was supposed to be there. Even after returning home to Colorado, that feeling would not go away.

I worked for KFC at the time, and there was no way that what I made was going to get me through or even to college. My mom was a single parent and did not have her green card. All she had was a Social Security card that allowed her to work. But without the green card, she could not find a great job because she was not a legal citizen yet. So although she worked tirelessly, we barely had enough.

My dad had abandoned my family when I was 14 years old, so I couldn't turn to him. The only thing I truly had was God and His Word. Psalm 23 resonated with me because in my eyes I truly believed the Lord is my Shepherd; I had no one else but him.

After graduating high school, I began to pray and ask God to provide for me to go to school. I read more verses like, *"If you abide in me, and my words abide in you, ask whatever you wish, and it will be done for you." (John 15:7)* As I read these verses, I felt persuaded inside that they were true, and I believed them.

The summer before I attended SAGU, I worked very hard at my job. Deep down inside, though, I knew it was not going to be enough. Each semester of SAGU was $8,000, and I only had a few hundred dollars. But I did not waver. I knew I was not chasing my dream, but the dream maker.

One day while I was at work, my boss told me "KFC gives scholarships to people who had been working for them for a year, all you have to do is submit a paper." Psalm 23 rang in my mind and I quickly turned in a paper sharing my story. Shortly after that, I was awarded a $10,000 scholarship.

This scholarship was broken down into $2,500 per semester, which was $5,000 per year. Now all I had left was $11,000 for the year. I was in communication with the financial aid at the school when all of a sudden, I couldn't get a hold of them anymore. I called and called, but no answer.

The clock was ticking, and I had about a week left before registration. Despite the financial need I still had, I could feel this persuasion in me to keep moving forward. I went to my youth pastor and asked him to buy me a one-way ticket to Texas. "Either it's God or it's not," I said, "but I must trust Him." So, my youth pastor bought me a $70 one-way ticket to Texas.

God did so many miraculous things while I was at SAGU that I cannot in one chapter begin to even explain it all. Throughout my time at SAGU I was not in need. As I kept meditating on His word and doing what it said, I was blessed in my doing. As it is written, *"But the one who looks into the perfect law, the law of liberty, and perseveres, being no hearer who forgets but a doer who acts, he will be blessed in his doing."* *(James 1:25)*

Money would literally just show up! Thousands of dollars would just appear in my account. Obviously, someone would feel compelled to give, but only as I kept trusting God. My faith in Christ birthed miracles in my life and in the lives of others.

For instance, one day while I was in the prayer room, a football player named Jared Hudgins came in and started sharing about all God had been doing in his life. As he spoke to my friends and I, I heard the Holy Spirit say, "tackle him."

Maybe I'm going crazy, I thought. But I heard it again: "tackle him." I looked at him as he was talking, and I could see his muscles bulging through the clothes he was wearing. Again, the voice said, "tackle him." I could feel this deep persuasion. It was not impulsive, just convincing.

Without any more thought, I lunged towards him. I could see his eyes get big, and his arms moved to the side as I hit him in the chest with my hands. Immediately, he began to speak in tongues for the first time. His face was filled with so much joy!

That year he set the record for tackles in the nation. He was playing like a man who had been endowed with power from On High! It was remarkable to watch.

Not too long after this incident I was told by the financial aid that I still owed $6,555 dollars for that semester and if I could not come up with the money, I had to leave. All my classes were dropped, and I decided to praise God in the midst of it all. I was reminded of Abraham, the father of faith. The Bible says, *"No unbelief made him waver concerning the promise of God, but he grew strong in his faith as he gave glory to God." (Romans 4:20)* Likewise, I too could not waver for I knew that me going to SAGU was God's plan and not my own. As I began to give God glory in the storm, I could feel my faith strengthen.

However, they finally told me that I had to leave. It was Friday when I was told this news. I had to decide either I was going to leave and try to find somewhere to go or I could stay because I could still feel that persuasive trust in my heart. I spoke to my dorm pastor and asked if I could stay for the weekend, and she agreed.

I continued to praise God throughout the weekend. My friends were also praying for me. When Monday came, I woke up and headed to the prayer room. I would have normally attended chapel, but I was afraid they'd kick me out.

I sneakily went by the chapel and headed towards the prayer room when suddenly, I saw that same football player that I'd tackled in the prayer room come out of the doors. He had blood dripping down his arm. Apparently, he picked a little scab and blood just poured out of it.

I asked him "Are you ok?" He looked at me and said, "Yes." I followed him to the bathroom just to make sure. When we went into the bathroom and he looked at me and asked me, "How you doing Gloire? Is everything ok?"

I responded, "Yeah everything is fine except I owe like 6,300 dollars." Without skipping a beat, he said, "I'll pay for it." I looked at him, stunned. He then called his mom, moved over his stocks, and wrote me a check for $6,555 dollars!

In this case, my faith produced the results I was believing for. Now my faith hasn't always produced the right results. There were times I was duped into believing the most foolish things because the gift of faith can make one susceptible to believing anything, if it's immature.

For example, when I was going to SAGU, I was believing God was going to provide for everything. One day, I got an email from someone saying that they had a fortune and they felt led by God to give it to me.

Without thinking, I believed this was God. I spoke to Katie, who I was courting at the time, about this amazing news. To my surprise, she was not as ecstatic about the news. She warned me that it may be a scam.

But I'm a believer! I thought. I disregarded the warning and I kept trusting that this was real until I had given these people pretty much all my info except for my social. It's a good thing Katie was persistent; she kept warning me until I dug deeper and found out there were many people getting the same emails. The stories were horrific, because people had given their bank account information and had lost everything.

The Bible puts it this way, *"Desire without knowledge is not good, and whoever makes haste with his feet misses his way." (Proverbs 19:2)* **I had a deep desire to please God but I did not have enough wisdom to sustain my desire, so sometimes I missed the way God was leading me.**

Maturity for the gift of faith is realizing that your gift is incomplete without the other gifts. Many people who have the gift of faith feel the need to force others into taking the same steps as them instead of teaching them how and allowing the Spirit of God to mature them. The gift of faith is not the greatest gift; it is only one of the many great gifts.

CHAPTER 31

The Gift of Healing

Out of all the gifts on this list, healing to me is the one that I've personally had the hardest time understanding. Sometimes when I prayed for people I would, since I had the gift of faith, try to believe them into being healed. I hardly saw anyone truly get healed this way.

Recently, though, I had a chance to see firsthand the gift of healing in operation. I took a trip to Texas to minister at a conference called Epic Fire led by my friend Stacey Jones. My friend Matt Daniels and I were asked to speak at the conference. Matt spoke on the first day, which was a Friday. He spoke about intimacy with God.

Before he spoke, he cultivated the atmosphere through praise. As he started speaking, he felt as though God wanted to heal people, so he said, "Is there anyone who has any pain in their right shoulder?" Several people raised their hands and he called them forward. What happened next blew my mind.

He had them pray for each other one by one and command the pain to leave. One by one, each person got healed. I was shocked! He didn't even have them pray a long prayer. Through the praise, we were all saturated in the presence of God and anything is possible in His presence.

But shoulders being healed was only the beginning. I saw things in that room that I had never seen before. For the next two hours, 90 percent of everyone who got prayed for was healed. He looked up at the chairs where the kids were sitting and he saw a kid who had a knee brace on and asked him what had happened. The teen went on to explain how three months prior, he was in a car accident and messed up his knee.

At that moment there was another teen right next to him up front who came up for healing as well. Matt told the teen who was sitting in the chair to come down and pray for the other kid up front. Then Matt said, "By the time you walk down here, your knee is going to be completely healed." The teen responded and walked around the chairs to the front and sure enough, all the pain in his knee left!

The young man then proceeded to pray for his friend and his friend's shoulder got completely healed. After this, Matt asked if there were people who had one leg shorter than the other, and he pulled up a chair. A man responded and came and sat in the chair. We found something for him to prop his legs on so we could physically see the difference. Sure enough, one leg was shorter than the other.

Matt then commanded his leg to grow, and with my own eyes I saw his leg grow back! The man who was sitting there felt it grow as well. When he stood up he told us all about how his back pain was gone and how he could sense the difference.

At this point, everyone was pretty much up and wanted to be involved. There were kids in the room and since Matt was having people pray, they all wanted to be a part of it. Hardly anyone was sitting down anymore.

There was a teenager who had a bone sticking out by his kneecap. The teenager talked about how he would always feel pain. Matt grabbed a kid who was about six years old and brought him. He then asked him to put his hand on that knee area. The kid did, and Matt helped him pray. He said, "Bone, go back to your place, and be healed." The kid was shy, so Matt prayed it for him. As he removed his hand, the bone went back into its place.

The teen said he felt no more pain!!! I couldn't believe my eyes. It didn't stop here though; Matt proceeded to have the kids call people on their phones and we were going to pray for them to be healed. The kids called parents, aunts, grandparents, and anyone they knew who was sick. One by one, God healed each person on the phone.

From this experience, I gathered two things about healing. One, the people seeking healing did not need to have great faith. **If someone believed, everyone had a chance to receive.** Secondly, either the person facilitating the healing or someone else in the room needed to know God intimately.

There's a great story in the Bible of a man being healed because of the faith of his friends. Jesus was teaching one day, and many teachers and Pharisees gathered around him. The Bible says that *"the power of the Lord was with him to heal." (Luke 5:17)*

This power was from the Holy Spirit. The word power here is the Greek word *dynamis*. This is the same word used by Luke in Acts 1:8, when he describes the Holy Spirit empowering the disciples.

As He continued teaching,

"...behold, some men were bringing on a bed a man who was paralyzed, and they were seeking to bring him in and lay him before Jesus, but finding no way to bring him in, because of the crowd, they went up on the roof and let him down with his

bed through the tiles into the midst before Jesus. And when he saw their faith, he said, 'Man, your sins are forgiven you'" (Luke 5:18-20).

Jesus forgave this man, and to prove to the Pharisees He had the power to forgive, He commanded the man to get up, take his mat, and go home. Notice though, the Bible says Jesus saw "their faith." In other words, if someone has some level of faith, God can move in a situation.

Someone who is mature in the gift of healing will never try to force healing on an individual. They know that the healer is God and they are conduits that God uses to manifest His will on the earth. Furthermore, their ability to operate in this gift flows from a place of deep intimacy with God.

CHAPTER 32

Healing and Deliverance

The word for healing in 1 Corinthians 12:9 is the Greek word *therapeuo*. Therapeuo is used a total of 42 times in the New Testament and is the most commonly used word for healing. It is connected to the English word *therapy*. It means to heal, serve, cure, to care for the sick, and on some occasions cast out demons.[1]

In the Gospel of Luke, Luke tells a story about a lady who had a spirit of infirmity. A spirit of infirmity means there was a demonic entity that was causing her sickness. For us to truly understand how Jesus healed her, we need to look at Luke 13:10-17.

"Now he was teaching in one of the synagogues on the Sabbath. And behold, there was a woman who had had a disabling spirit for eighteen years. She was bent over and could not fully straighten herself. When Jesus saw her, he called her over and said to her, 'Woman, you are freed from your disability.' And he laid his hands on her, and immediately she was made straight, and she glorified God. But the ruler of the synagogue, indignant because Jesus had healed on the Sabbath, said to the people, 'There are six days in which work ought to be done. Come on those days and be healed, and not on the Sabbath day.' Then the Lord answered him, 'You hypocrites! Does not each of you on the Sabbath untie his ox or his donkey from the manger and lead it away to water it? And ought

not this woman, a daughter of Abraham whom Satan bound for

eighteen years, be loosed from this bond on the Sabbath day?' As

he said these things, all his adversaries were put to shame, and all

the people rejoiced at all the glorious things that were done by him."

In the beginning of the passage we find out that Jesus is teaching in a synagogue, which is a place where believers would congregate. In verse 11, Luke points out that this woman was disabled, but he adds that this disability is due to a demonic spirit that had caused her pain for 18 years!

Jesus, told her, *"...Woman, you are freed from your disability." (Luke 13:12)* Notice how Jesus did not say be healed but specifically said you are freed from your disability. She did not need healing from a natural ailment, she needed deliverance from a demonic onslaught.

Later, in the passage Jesus makes a startling revelation. The Pharisees were trying to rebuke Jesus for healing on the Sabbath, and he made this statement, *"...ought not this woman, a daughter of Abraham whom Satan bound for eighteen years, be loosed from this bond on the Sabbath day?" (Luke 13:16)*

Jesus calls her a daughter of Abraham, a believer, and he accredits the ailment to the devil. **This is what's known as a spirit of infirmity: a sickness of any kind brought about from an attack of the devil and his demons.**

I want to share a story about two of my friends who were delivered from a spirit of infirmity and barrenness.

EGAN AND KYLIE BLACK

Both of us were raised Catholic, Egan a little more involved than me. He was baptized and received his First Communion in the Catholic Church. When we met, I was not really involved in anything religious. I believed in God, but I now understand that I did not know God. Egan was a brand-new Christian and was in a stage of repentance, actively working on turning away from sin and living a better life.

Before we met, I had experienced some strange things. In high school, my mom dated a man who owned a pawn shop. I spent a lot of time in the pawn shop, and even worked there. This pawn shop was located about an hour from a Native American Reservation, and a lot of the customers were Native American. I would see people come in and pawn ceremonial artifacts as well as other sacred things. Some of these things if not picked back up would be hung as decorations in the house I lived in, and this is when I started having strange experiences.

One night, I was sleeping and happened to awake. Toward the end of my bedroom, there seemed to be a dark figure standing still. I assumed I was still partially sleeping so I took a moment to fully open my eyes and be sure I was awake. Rather than the figure disappearing as I assumed it would, it was still there, just standing. All I could see was a silhouette of a man in a long trench coat, wearing a wide-brimmed hat, and boots. I sat in my bed, and just stared in disbelief, unsure of what to do. Finally, I got out of bed and slowly walked towards the light switch that was located in between the figure and myself. As I flipped the switch on, the figure disappeared, leaving nothing but an empty wall where it had been standing.

Over the next month, I would see this figure in my room at night. It was nearly the same experience each night, except as the month progressed, the figure would inch closer and closer to me. The last night I saw him, I awoke to him standing over me on my bed, staring down at me. This experience was terrifying, but I was too afraid to tell my Mom or anyone else because I didn't want them to assume, I was crazy. The night he stood over me, though, I finally had enough and knew I had to do something. The following morning, I called my sister who was the only person I knew that talked about God. She prayed with me over the phone, and from then on, I no longer physically saw the figure, and would only dream about him.

About a year later, I met Egan. This was a low time in my life because I spent a lot of time partying and drinking. I had always preferred not sleeping in a dark room, but one-night Egan turned the light off, and I felt terrified. I made him turn the light back on and that's how we slept. After that night, I moved us to the living room to sleep where we could make a bed in front of a large TV, and I was never in the dark. Both Egan and I started seeing and feeling something in the house. It was the same dark figure I thought I had left in the past. The same man, or better yet, silhouette with the long coat, large hat, and black boots. We would see him in the house, feel him standing near us as we slept, and hear footsteps when no one was there.

One night, I had a dream about a Native American woman. She came to me in my sleep begging for help. She told me there was an entity in the house and that she was trapped there. She told me that Egan and I needed to get it out but that he would stop at nothing to stay, and we needed to be quick and careful. I woke up and immediately told Egan about my dream. He told me he had an idea, and we would speak to someone about it the next day.

In the morning, he contacted a friend and known medicine man in the community. The man invited us to his house to share our experiences and decide what he would be able to do to help us. That evening, Egan and I went to visit this man and his wife and to share the torment we had been experiencing. I told him the same story I shared here, starting with what happened when I was in high school and what had been happening more recently. As I spoke, he and his wife paused and looked at each other, the wife saying, "Are you seeing what I'm seeing?" and the husband nodded. They looked and me and told me they knew what was harassing us, and that it had been attached to me since high school.

They told us it was a spirit that causes death. They shared some stories of people driving and swerving to stop from hitting a person on the highway and dying in the process. It was known to them as an angel of death and told us something needed to be done about it right away. They had just hosted a sweat, which is a ceremony the Blackfeet people use for a variety of reasons. Even though they just completed one, they told us this was an emergency and would need to have another one, specifically for us. We had a week to prepare. Preparations included buying material in certain colors, tobacco, and other things to be used in the ceremony, and as a gift to the man and his wife.

Finally, the day had come, and we were on our way from town to the location of the sweat. We had been warned that strange things would happen to deter us from making it there. There were several things that had happened which I struggle to remember now, so many years later. I do remember one of the issues was car problems and I was barely able to make it there on time. I never had any problems with that car before or after that. I got there, we had the sweat, and Egan and I were told the entity was gone.

Fast-forward several months and Egan and I were living in Arizona. We had started going to church together and it was at this time that I was saved and felt the fire of the Holy Spirit. I completely felt on-fire for God. Again, strange things started happening. Egan worked graveyard shifts at the time and I didn't have a phone. My only way to contact him was by Facebook Messenger by using my laptop. We had been talking and I fell asleep on my bed with the computer in front of me and the light on. I woke up feeling like I was being watched. I tried calling my two dogs to my bed as they usually slept with me, but they just stared at me and wouldn't move.

I then messaged Egan who was at work and told him how I felt. It was probably between 2 AM and 3 AM. He told me it was strange that I had shared this information with him because moments before he had a weird daydream of me sleeping, and demons standing around our bed watching me. He told me just to pray, read my Bible, and we would talk to some of our friends about it in the morning.

The following morning, we contacted some friends from church and told them what happened. We continued to experience feelings of something evil in our apartment. Our friends came over to our house to pray with us and as a test, I asked the husband to see if he could tell what side of the bed I slept in, as that's where we felt the most uncomfortable. He walked right over to my side of the bed and said, "Here. This is where I feel it the most."

The husband and wife prayed at our apartment and had a strong feeling the reason we were being harassed had to do with Native American religion. They felt someone had put some kind of curse on us and their solution was for us to gather anything anyone gave us that practices Native American religion, even if it was from someone, we considered a friend.

We worked on gathering things over the next few days and had planned to meet our friends at their house later that week to pray and burn everything. During those few days, both the husband and Egan had dreams about Native American men basically claiming Egan and I. One day, our friend and his wife were in Walmart and saw these two big Native men who happened to be the same men he dreamt about, that he also didn't know, and had never seen before besides in his dream. They followed our friends around Walmart for a while.

The next day, Egan and I were walking into a building, and a truck drove by in front of us, and some type of liquid landed on my husband's arm, but quickly disappeared. We both looked up to see who had just passed by, and it was two big Native men that matched the description of the guys our friend dreamt about and saw in Walmart. The next day, we got all of the stuff, went to our friend's house, and burned everything.

We prayed for any curses to be broken off and repented for previously participating in Native American ceremonies. After doing this, we did not battle with anymore scary or intimidating spirits. This was really one of the first times we experienced the power of God, and the authority we have that has been given to us as children of God. Between the time we attended the sweat and the end of this experience nearly a year later, we were both saved and were both on fire for God.

The rest of our story takes place over an eight-year period and highly centers around us wanting to be parents but being unable to do so. When Egan and I met, I was unsaved, and Egan was a new Christian. We met in December 2008 in Montana and moved in together in Arizona in February 2009. I was 18 years old and he was 21. We were madly in love, like the love you see in the movies. I didn't even know this kind of love could be real or could be something I could experience being so young.

Even though at the time we knew we shouldn't live together, we chose to anyway and didn't really feel bad or convicted about it. After we got saved, we started feeling convicted about living together and being intimate outside of marriage. We knew we wanted to spend our lives together and so in April 2010, just over a year and at the young ages of 19 and 22, we got married.

I came from a family of young moms and always wanted to be a mom myself. Although we hadn't really been careful about avoiding pregnancy, I decided I was ready to start a family, so we continued to not use any type of birth control. When I think back now, it really was by the grace of God that I didn't get pregnant then. We struggled so much, especially financially, that bringing a child into the world would have been so challenging for us.

However, we did spend the rest of our marriage not using birth control. After a few years of not getting pregnant we started to worry something was wrong. I went in and did some different kinds of tests. They checked my uterus and Fallopian tubes and when they couldn't find any issues, recommended Egan do some tests as well. Everything came back normal for both of us health wise.

The doctor considered my slow thyroid as a problem and recommended I get my thyroid levels normal for a year straight and see if I got pregnant. I followed their advice but had my levels in a normal range for several years, and still, nothing was happening. During this time, Egan and I had talked to both Gloire, and his brother-in-law and our friend, Daniel. Both were getting words from God that I would one day be pregnant, and I would be pregnant several times.

Our seventh year of marriage rolled around, and Egan and I were really, really, ready to be parents. We had always talked about adopting and wanted to adopt even before we questioned fertility. One day we picked up this beautiful baby girl from a nurturing center. She had been abandoned and was 5 ½ weeks old. We took her home and fell in love with her. During the year it took to adopt her, several things happened.

During that year I chose to go through deliverance with Gloire. Egan and I met Gloire in our church and went through the process of deliverance. As we prayed there were several spirits, we felt had been oppressing me. One of them I felt come out of my womb. It was a strange but exciting experience.

A couple months later, Gloire had set us up with a time to talk with and be prayed over by his friend who was a prophetess. She prayed and gave us some words she got from God. Towards the end she asked if we had any questions. I loved being a Mom to our little girl, but still couldn't shake the desire I had to be pregnant. I asked her if Egan and I would ever conceive children, and she immediately answered, "She laughed and said 9 years 9 months, you will be pregnant this year." It had been 9 years of us trying to have a child and she prophesied that it is significant because it's connected to 9 months. She told us the time would be significant and I would actually be pregnant very soon. This was the winter of 2018 and, in the summer, that year, I discovered I was pregnant!

God was with us, reassuring us throughout all the years we struggled with doubts, so why would he abandon us when I finally got pregnant? In July 2018, on a Saturday, I was having these weird daydreams where I was standing in the gym at work (I teach middle school P.E.), and the 7th graders I had the previous year were in 8th grade. They were standing around me asking about my baby, and I could see that I was pregnant. I had this daydream so many times that day and just thought I was hoping.

The next morning on Sunday, Gloire sent us a video message saying he had a dream about us. In this dream he told us he saw me, and I was pregnant. He then told us, "Your child is going to be great. The child you have in your womb is going to be great." He then told us our daughter who we had adopted earlier in the year was toddler age and at the time she was a little over a year old. He told us we should probably take a test because I was probably pregnant, or I would be soon.

After we watched his video, Egan and I just looked at each other. I told Egan that Gloire's video was confirmation that I needed to take a pregnancy test because I had been having weird daydreams the day before that I was pregnant. We went to church and afterwards, I took a test, and it was positive!!

After years and years of fear, doubt, and hopelessness, I was finally pregnant. I thought back to every time God gave us a word. Every time He told us His timing, not ours. Every time He had someone reassure us it would happen. We prayed so much and just months before I got pregnant, we felt something lift from my body, specifically my womb, and was promised by a prophet that God had a plan, and we would conceive. God is a healer and a deliverer, and He does things in His time, but He also doesn't want us to sit on our hands when He makes us a promise. We must take an active role in getting His promises.

He promised us we would conceive children, and for years, we sat on that promise thinking, "What the heck? You said it would happen. Where it this baby You promised?" When we started taking an active role in getting what He promised us, going through deliverance, we finally received the promise. God doesn't just speak to speak. He doesn't give promises just to make us feel good. He is good and He means what He says. He will break down walls, heal hearts, bodies, and relationships, but we need to act. We need to move when He says move. We need to get out from under oppression. We need deliverance!

CHAPTER 33

The Working of Miracles

There've been many movies, stories, and books about miracles. Whether it be in the medical/scientific field or day-to-day life, people from every creed, color, and background have either experienced what they call a miracle or have heard of miraculous stories. When talking about miracles, though, one must differentiate between healing and the miraculous.

In the New Testament, there are different words that help expand on the word healing. There's *sozo,* which means salvation from one's sins and from an enemy. Then there's *therapeu*, which means to heal, serve, cure, to care for the sick and on some occasions healing through casting out demons. Lastly, there's the word *Iaomai*. Iaomai is the power of God, which releases miraculous healing and casting out of demons.[1]

To define the working of miracles, we must look at the words "working" and "miracles" in the Greek. According to Strong's concordance, the word "working" in this passage in the Greek is *energéma*, which means "energizings ("operations"), focusing on the results of God's "energy" (power) in people living in His faith.[2] Therefore, in this context, "working" actually means to be empowered or energized by God as you live for Him and are used for his operations.

Miracles, on the other hand, is the word *dunamis* in the Greek. It means the "ability to perform;" for the believer, power to achieve by applying the Lord's inherent abilities." [3] **It is power through God's ability.** Whereas workings refer to being energized by God for a task, miracles refer to having God's abilities while doing the tasks.

I have countless stories of miracles; from the way I was born to finding my wife and finishing college. But in this book, I'm only going to talk about two miraculous events that happened to me. The first event literally happened while I've been writing this book. As I've been writing this book God has allowed me to experience the gifts of the Holy Spirit one by one before or during the chapters on those specific gifts. It's been nothing short of amazing.

In 2018, my wife and I started out the year rough. Financially we had nothing. I was working two jobs: I was an egg inspector and I was also in full-time ministry. The egg inspection job was part time job, and they initially said I would work ten hours per week. This turned out to be a stretch from reality. I worked about ten hours a week for a month and then I did not work again for nearly eight months.

Now the full-time ministry job for my church didn't not pay me. Occasionally someone would give me several hundred dollars, but this was just enough to get by. I'm so thankful that one of our friends took us in and allowed us to stay in her basement for free or we could have been in a worse situation.

Being that this was my first time being a father, I could feel the pressures of leading a family. On top of that, my wife was pregnant with our second child, so we were about to become a family of four. It was during this time that I got a job offer from a friend from church.

Instead of praying over the job offer like I normally would, I just took the job. The job was to be a mail carrier to the rural part of the town in Shelby and Galata, Montana. I would deliver mail to people and places that the regular U.S post system didn't go.

From the very beginning, I found myself struggling to figure out the job. My boss Danelle was an amazing teacher, but we had experienced one of the worst snowstorms that winter and it was hard for me to remember the routes.

After almost three months' worth of on and off training, I finally figured out how to do the short days which were Tuesdays, Thursdays, and Saturdays. Then I was able to start taking a couple of long days.

This is where things made a turn for the worst. My boss had to supply her own vehicles for the job, so she had an almost 20-year-old van and a Jeep. The Jeep was my favorite because it had great big tires, which were perfect for the country roads. The van was my least favorite. When you drove it on the dirt road, dust flew into the vehicle even if the windows were up. This made it hard to breathe and see, so I wore a dust mask and on occasion my sunglasses, so the dust didn't fly into my eyes.

She had told me that Mondays were the hardest days because mail would accumulate during the weekend. Monday, July 16th, 2018 was my first Monday and probably my third long day by myself. I remember getting to work and seeing all the mail I had to deliver and trying to keep a positive attitude. After gathering all my mail at the Shelby post office, I headed out. I stopped by one of my first stops and spoke to two awesome people for a bit, then I continued my route.

Everything that could go wrong seemed to have gone wrong. I was driving the van because the jeep needed to be repaired. The seatbelt in the van had been cut, so I was without a seatbelt. As I was driving, I realized I forgot my sunglasses. The whole vehicle was filled with dust but thank God I had my dust mask.

As I continued to drive, the van got hot inside. There's no air conditioning, nor do you want to turn it on because of the dust. Normally we don't really roll the window down either because it helps circulate the dust in the van, but I was too hot, so I rolled it down some. Not too long after I rolled down the window, some mail flew out my window while I was driving into the fields.

There was no way to get that mail, so I was glad that it had just been junk mail. I was almost in Galata, where the second post office was, but a train caused me to be late.

When I finally arrived, I went inside the post office and saw that I had even more mail to deliver. I still tried to encourage myself. *Five more hours and then I'm done,* I told myself. I headed out on my route from Galata, delivered some more mail, and came back to pick up the last of the mail for my last route. I was about to take my last turn towards a place Montana called Sweet Grass Hills when I had a sense that I should roll my window all the way down, so I did.

After rolling down my window I turned onto Minor Cooley road. *Only an hour and a half left*, I thought to myself. Now down this road, there's a giant S-curve that transitions you to a T in the road. There's no sign that indicates there's a giant S-curve coming, but they put a sideways T-sign where the S-curve is coming, making it seem like the road continues straight when in actuality it turns.

By the time I realized that I was turning it was too late. I tried to correct my mistake and I turned too hard to the left. There was fresh gravel laid out. so, I began to slide. Not thinking, I pushed the brakes hard and tried to turn the wheels to the right. This perpetuated sliding, but now I was sliding the other way and headed straight for the ditch. I hit the ditch, and then I turned my wheel back to the left and began to slide in the ditch towards the passenger side.

Suddenly, I came to an abrupt stop and the van began to roll. Both my hands were lifted and off the steering wheel. It seemed like time stopped in this moment. As the van flipped into the passenger side and continued to flip into the driver's side, my window hit the ground, and it was as if someone pulled me out. My body turned from facing the steering wheel to facing the passenger window.

All of me fit perfectly through the window as I got thrown out the van. I hit the back of my head with force, but it felt like I hit a pillow. I then somersaulted backwards and stood to my feet all in one motion. As I did, I saw the van finishing half a roll. No broken bone. No concussion. A little tiny scrape here and there. Momentarily I had pain in my left ankle, but God healed that. This was nothing short of a miracle!

According to some statistics, nearly 30 percent of deaths during a car accident are caused by ejection.[4] The percentage goes up if there's no seatbelt. So according to statistics I should be dead, but God has a plan for my life!

One thing should be clear though; miracles are signs that should point to Jesus. Just because you've experienced a miracle or performed a miracle does not mean you know the Lord. Jesus addresses this when he is sharing about those who thought that because they flowed in their gifting, it meant they knew Him.

Jesus puts it this way,

"Many will say to me on that day, 'Lord, Lord, did we not prophesy in your name and in your name drive out demons and in your name perform many miracles?' Then I will tell them plainly, 'I never knew you. Away from me, you evildoers!'" (Matthew 7:22-23)

How is it that these people did all these things and yet Jesus says I never knew you? The word *knew* here has to do with intimacy. Jesus is saying "I never knew you *intimately*." This is fitting for all the gifts. **One mustn't always conclude that what they do proves who they are. What you do should be a byproduct of who you are.** Doing must be from a place of being or else all that you've done in this life will amount to nothing in eternity.

As a summation of the gifts of the Holy Spirit, I've included a test you can take on the back of the book.

CHAPTER 34

The Parental Gifts: My Body

I grew up in a single-parent home for most of my life. When I was born, my mom told me my dad did not believe I was his, so for pretty much the first six years of my life, I grew up fatherless. My dad came into my life when I was about to turn seven, but he did not last. When I was 14, he abandoned my whole family again.

Although I was taken in by a Hispanic family called the Lucero's, my mom still had to play the role of a mom and a dad. My dad leaving scattered the whole family, and we're still trying to repair the damage from it after 15 years.

Growing up in a fatherless home affects every aspect of an individual's life. Infants who grow up fatherless can have problems with weight gain. Many children who grow up in fatherless homes will experience teen pregnancy, may become a juvenile, not value school, have suicidal tendencies, gang affiliations, and so much more.[1]

One thing that's not mentioned here is gender dysphoria. This is when people are dealing with gender confusion. The person might think he's a girl when he's really a boy, and vice versa. Society has tried to change the definition to make it fit the social norms of today, but the reality is that fatherless homes can cause children to not know their identity. (A good book about this topic is *How I Came Out and Stayed Out,* By Astacia Jones.)

Furthermore, according to many statistics on fatherlessness, many girls who do not have a father at home can become very promiscuous at a very young age.

"A study of 263 13- to 18-year-old adolescent women seeking psychological services found that the adolescents from father-absent homes were 3.5 times more likely to experience pregnancy than were adolescents from father-present homes."[2]

Clearly, sexual immorality can be tied to fatherlessness. **When a father is absent from a home, it can be filled with all kinds of dysfunction.**

But the opposite is also true. A house that has both parents present can produce children who are not immune to struggle, but because they have great support, they make better choices and may face less consequences.

God created the family unit to function in harmony. Did you know that there are three instances that God gives us His Spirit, and one has to do with family? The first instance of God giving us His Spirit is when you're born again, and His Spirit regenerates your spirit. Secondly, when you get baptized in the Spirit, God's Spirit takes full control of your life. Lastly, when you get married, God gives a portion of His Spirit (Malachi 2).

Malachi, which means messenger, was a prophet in the Old Testament. God, through Malachi, rebuked the Israelites for their unfaithfulness to Him, the law, and each other. One specific situation is found in Malachi 2. God addressed the Israelites' unfaithfulness to their spouses. He was mad because they had thrown away their wives through divorce.

"Did he not make them one, with a portion of the Spirit in their union? And what was the one God seeking? Godly offspring. So guard yourselves in your spirit, and let none of you be faithless to the wife of your youth" (Malachi 2:15).

This is powerful! This is why marriage is holy! God baptizes the married couple with His Spirit. God even gives the answer to why He does this. It says, "And what was the one God seeking? *Godly offspring.*" **In other words, your unity in marriage has direct implications as it relates to your children growing up godly.** I recommend that if your child is acting out, check your unity in your marriage.

It is true, however, that adversity helps to propel people to do incredible feats. For instance, who I am today is in part due to what I've faced. I had to learn perseverance, and it built character in me. I also developed an attitude that nothing was impossible with God because I was an impossible case that He solved.

On the other hand, the struggle is real. A lot of things I went through in life could have been avoided if my parents had both been there in a healthy way. I still at times find myself making mistakes just because there are certain things that having a father could have helped me know how to do.

For instance, being a husband, a father, and a provider. It took me a long time to navigate through this and a list of other feelings and situations in life. The crazy part of all this is God really made sure I still had a form of family after my parents separated; most people don't get this opportunity.

God put me with amazing people who temporarily filled the role of my parents. So, although I still had a longing for my dad and mom, I was connected with a Hispanic family who helped steward the heart of God in me. I gained a brother, sisters, cousins and aunts. I also gained responsibilities, as I was expected to do my part in the family. Having this system helped keep me out of a lot of trouble.

The church in Scripture is supposed to function like a family. When speaking to people about his earthly family, Jesus said,

"...Who is my mother, and who are my brothers?" And stretching out his hand toward his disciples, he said, "Here are my mother and my brothers! For whoever does the will of my Father in heaven is my brother and sister and mother" (Matthew 12:48-50).

According to Jesus, those who are doing God's will should be more of a family than even your own fleshly family.

When Paul speaks to the church in Corinth, there are many times where he addresses them as if they were his spiritual children. *"For though you have countless guides in Christ, you do not have many fathers. For I became your father in Christ Jesus through the gospel"* (1 Corinthians 4:15). According to Paul, his impartation of the gospel to the Corinthians made his relationship with them more of a parental relationship. But like any family, when parents are absent, dysfunction is present.

I believe the church has lost its function because the spiritual parents are divorced. In Ephesians 4:11-16, Paul talks about the gifts that are supposed to help the church mature into manhood. Paul says this about the gifts of Christ,

"And he gave the apostles, the prophets, the evangelists, the shepherds and teachers, to equip the saints for the work of ministry, for building up the body of Christ, until we all attain to the unity of the faith and of the knowledge of the Son of God, to mature manhood, to the measure of the stature of the fullness of Christ, so that we may no longer be children, tossed to and fro by the waves and carried about by every wind of doctrine, by human cunning, by craftiness in deceitful schemes. Rather, speaking the truth in love, we are to grow up in every way into him who is the head, into Christ, from whom the whole body, joined and held together by every joint with which it is equipped, when each part is working properly, makes the body grow so that it builds itself up in love" (Ephesians 4:11-16).

A husband was not made to function apart from his wife or a wife apart from her husband or children apart from their parents. Likewise, the apostles were not made to function without the prophets and the prophets were not made to function without the evangelists and the evangelists were not made to function without the pastors and the pastors were not made to function without the teachers and the church was not made to function without these offices in their proper roles.

If you look at the church today, you see dysfunction and disunity. Some Christians may make it into their calling, but not without the pain of growing up in a single parent home. **The church at large has operated like a single parent home.** What we normally see in our modern-day churches is a single parent figure, namely the pastor, trying to do the work of all the parents. As previously stated, when you grow up in a single parent home, life is difficult. You fall into so many traps and many people are never able to truly mature.

The answer to Christians maturing is given in Ephesians. Paul says,

"And he gave the apostles, the prophets, the evangelists, the shepherds and teachers, to equip the saints for the work of ministry, for building up the body of Christ, until we all attain to the unity of the faith and of the knowledge of the Son of God, to mature manhood to the measure of the stature of the fullness of Christ" (Ephesians 4:11-13).

Many people are under the assumption that only a special group of people get to hold these offices. Respectfully, I disagree. I firmly believe that although not everyone can lead at once, everyone has potential in the congregation to grow into one of these offices. In other words, in your congregation there are future apostles, prophets, evangelists, pastors, and teachers. And our job as leaders should be to guide them towards maturing in their God given potential, not to make them our subjects forever.

CHAPTER 35

The Hand Models the Parenting Gifts

If you've ever heard of what's commonly known as these "fivefold ministry" gifts, which I call the parenting gifts, you may also know the hand model that's been used to symbolize each function of these offices. I truly love this model because I feel that it's a practical tool that helps teach a concept in a way that even a child can understand it.

As I explain this model, I have added some things to it that I believe give even more clarity to these offices. Take one of your hands, open it up, and turn it around so the front of your palm is towards you.

Apostles

The thumb represents the apostle. He is away from all the other fingers because he is sent by God, many times to places that don't yet have any churches. He is the catalyst.

Your thumb is the only finger that can touch all the other fingers while facing them. When you attempt to touch the other fingers front to front the only way, they will touch is backwards. Because the apostle is sometimes alone, he may be used for a season prophetically (but this is not his office), to evangelize (but this is not his office), as a pastor (but this is not his office), to teach (but this is not his office).

Now all the other fingers can touch each other's side, and it's because they are meant to walk beside each other. Each finger can touch the thumb, but they are not the thumb. They too may be sent to a different place, although not in the same capacity as the thumb. The thumb can exist outside of being next to the other fingers for a longer time.

As you look at your thumb you can see that it is under all the other fingers. In the same way, the apostles should be serving these offices because their job in a church has to do with the foundation of the church. **The Apostles help to lift these other offices up by alleviating the pressures.**

A mature apostle should help plant churches, train leaders in a church, and work on the foundational legislation of the church (or assign someone to do so), making sure it's according to Scripture. Each office should preach the Word, but it may look different from one office to the next.

Prophet

The pointer finger in this model symbolizes the prophet. The pointer finger is the only finger that is connected to the side of the thumb. This is because they both have similar ministries. For instance, both the apostle and the prophet help with the foundation of the church. Beyond this, there are more differences than similarities.

One major difference is that the word "prophet" does not mean *sent*. This is not saying that prophets can't be sent as we see throughout the Old Testament, but it means that this is not their primary job. Just like your pointer finger points, this illustrates what a prophet's job is. Prophets point out what's right or wrong in individuals or church bodies, and they point people to Christ.

When you make a pointer finger, though, there are three fingers pointing back at you. **Always remember that a true prophet walks in humility and is first and**

foremost examining themselves and make sure what they speak, no matter how hard, is the truth in love. The fingers pointing at the prophet are also part of the other offices. Meaning, a healthy prophet is one who is checked on and in community with the other offices.

Evangelist

The next finger is the middle finger. This finger can be offensive and vulgar to many people. This symbolizes the evangelist. They are the messengers. Because they are more concerned with where your soul is going, they may speak truth in light of controversy.

Evangelists sometimes can be seen holding signs that may say "Turn or Burn". Yet this is not how I believe an evangelist was made to operate. **You see, the only way the middle finger is offensive is when it stands alone. But when it's standing next to the other fingers, its role is truly defined.**

The middle finger stretches out further than all the other fingers and it's because a healthy evangelist will stay close to the church and help the church reach out to the world.

Pastor

After the middle finger there's the ring finger. The ring finger exemplifies the Pastor. The ring finger is called the ring finger because when someone gets married, that's the finger they use to seal the covenant. A ring on that finger shows you're married.

The pastor's job likewise is to make sure people keep their covenant with God and with each other. Once you put that ring on that finger, it is until death do you part. This means you can't just divorce your spouse for any reason. The pastor and the congregation should be bound to each other until God either separates them or death does.

The marriage ring symbolizes unity and a new direction. In the same way, it's the pastor's job to unite the church body and to direct the body by setting the vision in the house.

Teacher

Finally, there's the pinky. The pinky is the smallest finger, but it is just as important as the other fingers and in some situations, it may be more important. The pinky is the only finger that can for almost everyone reaches into their ears and clean them out.

The pinky represents the teacher. The teacher's job is to make sure that the right doctrine is being taught in the house of the Lord. They want to make sure that people don't just hear whatever their itching ears want to hear.

Pinkies can help clean the smallest things. Sometimes they can help you reach into places that all the other fingers are too big to reach. The teacher's job is to find the cracks in the belief system people may have accumulated over the years due to bad study habits. They help them clean their attitudes and change perceptions that may be based on lies.

CHAPTER 36

The Apostle

The Heavenly Man

My wife and I were once led to a book called the *Heavenly Man* by Brother Yun, one of the starters of the underground church in China. This book changed our lives! While reading it, I couldn't help but connect with this man in a deep way. His passion for Christ ignited a fire in me!

As I grew up in the Lord, I couldn't really find my place in the church. Sometimes I would preach, but I did not feel like I was a pastor. Sometimes I would evangelize, but I did not feel like an evangelist. Other times I would prophesy, but I did not feel like a prophet. At other times I would teach, but I knew I was not a teacher.

I began to ask myself, *who am I? Where do I fit in the church?* This troubled me a little bit because I felt like I couldn't operate in my full potential until I discovered who I was.

One day I was praying with a prophetess on the phone and she suddenly stopped praying and began to read my thoughts. She said, "You've been asking who am I? The reason why you operate the way you do is because you are an apostle." As soon as she said this my whole life began to make sense.

But God knew I needed more confirmation so He allowed me to be put in a situation that would give me one more confirmation. One day while my wife and I were in New York City, we heard that Brother Yun was coming to Staten Island in New York. We were so elated we called a few of our friends and invited them to come with us.

When we got there, I couldn't believe my eyes. There was hardly anyone there! The church wasn't that big, so we found some seats in the very front and to my disbelief, Brother Yun was sitting right next to us. As service started, he went up and began to preach with his interpreter. It was powerful!

After he finished, the Lord put on my heart to go and bless his ministry. I approached him and gave him the Pentecostal handshake (this is when you take money and place it in the hand that you are going to shake the other person's hand with). At that moment, he began to prophesy over me and my wife, he shouted, "Apostles! Apostles!" His interpreter, who had walked a little bit away from him, turned around and headed back to where we were.

Upon the interpreter's arrival, Brother Yun grabbed mine and my wife's hand and he went on his knees. We followed suit. He began to prophesy, saying, "God has called you guys to be apostles to the nations; you're going to go to many places to preach His Word!" This was the last confirmation that I needed; I knew from that moment on that this was my calling!

What then is an apostle? As mentioned at the beginning of the book, the word apostle in the Greek is *apostolos*, which means "sent". **The very first apostle was Jesus himself.** The Hebrew writer puts it this way *"...consider Jesus, the apostle and high priest of our confession" (Hebrews 3:1).* There are countless mentions of Jesus being sent (apostolos) by the Father (Mt 15:24; Lk 4:18; Mt 10:40; Mk 9:37; Lk 9:48; 10:16).

It is He, Jesus, who commissioned the apostles in the New Testament, also known as the 12 disciples. Judas is included in the apostleship because in the Gospel of Luke, Jesus names him as one of the original 12 apostles. Throughout Jesus ministry he would send the apostles out to minister to the lost sheep of Israel.

An apostle, therefore, is someone who is a disciple of Jesus whom Jesus has sent to go to different places in the world to share the good news (the gospel). There are many ways that people have described the role of an apostle throughout the years, but I believe if we first look at what Scripture has to say, maybe we can get a better picture of an apostle today.

According to the Bible, an apostle helps establish the foundation of a church. As it is written,

"So, then you are no longer strangers and aliens, but you are fellow citizens with the saints and members of the household of God, built on the foundation of the apostles and prophets, Christ Jesus himself being the cornerstone" (Ephesians 2:19-20).

Some refute what was written in the prior paragraph by stating that Paul in this verse is really talking about the Christian faith as a whole and how it is established on the Old Testament "prophets" and New Testament "apostles." Although this is true, the message Paul was trying to get across in these verses is not Old Testament and New Testament; it is just the New Testament.

The reason being is because Paul mentions the prophets and apostles again in Ephesians, but this time he clarifies that it is their *present* ministry. He mentions the mystery of the Messiah, *"which was not made known to the sons of men in other generations as it has now been revealed to his holy apostles and prophets by the Spirit"* *(Ephesians 3:5).* By "sons of men in other generations", the text is clearly speaking of the Old Testament, but when he says "now", he is addressing today's present ministry.

Furthermore, as Paul is admonishing the church in Ephesus, he points out to them that they are part of the Christian family. Just like a family system has different roles, here in this passage Paul addresses the role that an apostle and prophet play in a church, which is foundational. Jesus is the Cornerstone, the one who holds the whole building (family) together.

The Ministry of An Apostle

In 1 Corinthians 4, Paul describes the ministry of an apostle. He starts the chapter by explaining to the church that the apostles should be regarded *"as servants of Christ and stewards of the mysteries of God"* (1 Corinthians 4:1). By "mysteries", the Scripture is referring to the doctrines of the gospel such as sanctification, purification, revelation, salvation through Christ.

Furthermore, as stewards, apostles must be found faithful. This is not based on man's judgment, but on what God reveals on the day Jesus reappears to the world. Paul continues on this thought process by explaining to the church that as a whole, no one should view themselves greater than another because what we've received has been graciously given to us.

But what I would call the encapsulation of the apostles' ministry is found in verses 9-13. Paul says this:

"For I think that God has exhibited us apostles as last of all, like men sentenced to death, because we have become a spectacle to the world, to angels, and to men. We are fools for Christ's sake, but you are wise in Christ. We are weak, but you are strong. You are held in honor, but we in disrepute. To the present hour we hunger and thirst, we are poorly dressed and buffeted and homeless, and we labor, working with our own hands. When reviled, we bless; when persecuted, we endure; when slandered, we entreat. We have become, and are still, like the scum of the world, the refuse of all things."

Wow! Does this mean if someone is an apostle, they may experience at times higher levels of persecution? Yes, I would say the apostolic mantle carries with it a higher level of responsibility only because what they do is foundational. This does not mean we all don't face trials; the Word says, *"Indeed, all who desire to live a godly life in Christ Jesus will be persecuted"* (2 Timothy 3:12).

Apostles are the initiators in the church building process. This means since they are starters and are sent sometimes to places no one else has been, the devil will launch a full assault on the apostle to make sure the foundation is not laid.

In reading 1 Corinthians 4:9-13 the word humility comes to mind. I believe a mature apostle is known for their humble posture in light of trials and tribulations. Truly all these offices must be humble, but it especially behooves the apostle to be humble.

This is so important that Jesus allowed an agent from Satan to be sent to Paul to keep him from being filled with conceit.

"So, to keep me from becoming conceited because of the surpassing greatness of the revelations, a thorn was given me in the flesh, a messenger of Satan to harass me, to keep me from becoming conceited" (2 Corinthians 12:7).

Signs of a True Apostle

We are living in the last days, so it is paramount for one to know the difference between a true apostle and a false apostle. For instance, in the Mormon faith, they falsely adhere to a form of the fivefold ministry. This, for many believers, is why when the fivefold is mentioned, it's hard for them to reconcile because in Mormonism they have the same model (or so it's thought).

The same name does not mean the same model. If a team is named after the Golden State Warriors and they fail to live up to who the Golden State Warriors see themselves to be, the Golden State Warriors do not shy away from their identity in light of this. Truly, the Scripture gives an accurate description of an apostle, one that can help us to clearly separate between the "super apostles" (as Paul refers to them) and the true apostles.

Paul addresses the difference between a true apostle and a false apostle throughout his writings because where truth is, lies try to be present. Paul does this in hopes to deter these erroneous allegations that people were making about his apostleship. Paul states,

"I have been a fool! You forced me to it, for I ought to have been commended by you. For I was not at all inferior to these super-apostles, even though I am nothing.

The signs of a true apostle were performed among you with utmost patience, with

signs and wonders and mighty works" (2 Corinthians 12:11-12).

By "signs", I don't believe Paul is focused necessarily just "signs and wonders and mighty works." Rather, I believe it's the accumulation of passages before this, such as 2 Corinthians 4:9-13, where he talks about the humble nature of an apostle, even if they're reviled.

Furthermore, in 1 Corinthians Paul states, *"If to others I am not an apostle, at least I am to you, for you are the seal of my apostleship in the Lord" (1 Corinthians 9:2).* By seal here, Paul is referring to the fact that his conduct, devotion, and affection towards them should be proof to them that indeed he is an apostle because he had been like a father to them.

Essentially, a true apostle must believe in and only proclaim Christ. They must walk in humility and be triumphantly meek. Under God's authority, they must execute His Kingdom by being His manifesto, His written proclamation of His kingdom coming and His Kingdom here.

Now some would state that a major requirement for apostleship is seeing Christ. Understandably, it is important for one to get a revelation of their calling from God (Galatians) but this is true for all the offices. The assumption that one must see Christ is based off 1 Corinthians 9:1: *"Am I not free? Am I not an apostle? Have I not seen Jesus our Lord? Are not you my workmanship in the Lord?" (1 Corinthians 9:1)*

If indeed the requirements for being an apostle is to see Christ, then many people after Jesus' resurrection should be considered apostles. For Paul writes,

"For I delivered to you as of first importance what I also received: that Christ died for our sins in accordance with the Scriptures, that he was buried, that he was raised on the third day in accordance with the Scriptures, and that he appeared to Cephas, then to the twelve. Then he appeared to more than five hundred brothers at one time, most of whom are still alive, though some have fallen asleep. Then he appeared to James, then to all the apostles. Last of all, as to one untimely born, he appeared also to me. For I am the least of the apostles, unworthy to be called an apostle, because I persecuted the church of God" (1 Corinthians 15:3-9).

According to Paul, over 500 people saw the resurrected Christ. Does this mean all 500+ people were apostles? If we follow the logic of those who would say "one must see the resurrected Christ to be an apostle," we must conclude that it is true that there were over 500 apostles who are no longer here because Jesus only appeared to a special group of people. Not only this, but there have been countless Muslims, Hindus, and others who have come to Christ through seeing Jesus. Does this mean they all are now apostles? I do not believe this is the case.

CHAPTER 37

The Prophet

My wife and I can hardly remember a time in our life that we did not consult with a prophet or a prophetess to confirm what the Lord had spoken to us, especially when we had to make difficult decisions for ourselves and our family. There are countless stories of financial breakthroughs, our children's lives being spared, family members being rescued from a life of despair, friends saved from marrying people who were going to be abusive, friends who were hopeless finding hope, and so much more.

The Bible says, *"For the Lord GOD does nothing without revealing his secret to his servants the prophets" (Amos 3:7).* This verse is amazing to me because God is sovereign; He does not need us and yet he includes us because He wants us. This verse also truly shows our need for the prophetic. **A church that does not have a prophetic voice can become spiritually dead and blind because, in a sense, they silence a part of the voice of God that would enable them to see what's ahead.**

Prophets in the Old Testament had many responsibilities. They were the advisors of kings, messengers of God, spiritual leaders, warriors, teachers of the Word, and much more (Judges 4 & 5, 1 Kings 22:6, Jeremiah, Daniel, Exodus 4:11-12, Isaiah 6).

The word "prophet" in Hebrew has two connotations. The first one is *nabi,* which means "a spokesman or a speaker." The next one is *ro'eh,* which means "seer". Samuel makes this more clear when he writes, *"Formerly in Israel, when a man went to inquire of God, he said, "Come, let us go to the seer," (for today's "prophet" was formerly called a seer)" (1 Samuel 9:9).*

Therefore, a prophet is someone who sees what God shows them and is the mouthpiece of God here on earth. But some would suggest that all the prophets ceased with the death of John the Baptist. People who believe this come to this conclusion based on this verse, *"For all the Prophets and the Law prophesied until John" (Matthew 11:13).*

To better understand this verse, however, let's look at the entire passage. John the Baptist was just arrested by King Herod because he rebuked him for taking his brother's wife. While in prison, it seems as though John faced some uncertainty about Jesus. John sends his disciples to ask Jesus, *"Are you the one who is to come, or shall we look for another?" (Matthew 3).* This statement shows that John was a man like any of us. Just like us, sometimes he dealt with doubts about Jesus being who He says He is.

Jesus does not respond back by rebuking John. Rather, He tells the man who came asking him this question,

> *"Go and tell John what you hear and see: the blind receive their sight and the lame walk, lepers are cleansed and the deaf hear, and the dead are raised up, and the poor have good news preached to them. And blessed is the one who is not offended by me" (Matthew 11:4-6).*

Why did Jesus respond this way? Two reasons: one, this is the assimilation of the gospel. Secondly, Jesus' statement is referenced in Isaiah, a book that John would have been familiar with since Isaiah 40 speaks of John's ministry. This is what he quotes to the Pharisees when they questioned who he was (John 1:21). Jesus therefore, through this statement, showed John that what He was doing testifies of who he is (Isaiah 42:1-6).

But Jesus did not stop here. After the messenger went back to tell John what Jesus said, Jesus began to honor John. Some may have thought that after John questioned if Jesus was the Messiah, Jesus would have used his failure as a lesson so no one else would fall into the same thought process. Instead, Jesus says this: *"Truly, I say to you, among those born of women there has arisen no one greater than John the Baptist. Yet the one who is least in the kingdom of heaven is greater than he" (Matthew 11:11).*

Take in this verse for a minute. Jesus said there was no one born of woman who was greater than John! Jesus was born of a woman, yet it was divine conception. Nonetheless, Jesus elevated John in the natural as one greater than Himself outside the Kingdom of God.

Continuing with this thought, Jesus says, *"Yet the one who is least in the kingdom of heaven is greater than he" (Matthew 11:11).* Jesus inaugurated the Kingdom of God, so He of course is greater than John. But here we begin to see a divide between John's ministry and the ministry brought forth from Jesus.

The next verse says, *"From the days of John the Baptist until now, the Kingdom of Heaven has suffered violence, and the violent take it by force" (Matthew 11:12).* This is not saying the Kingdom of Heaven was the one under attack, but that "from the days"--meaning beginning of John's ministry--the Kingdom of Heaven has begun to advance forcefully through healing, casting out demons, the blind seeing, the dead being raised, and so forth. "And the violent take it by force" means that those who were healed, delivered, raised from the dead, have violently fiercely grabbed a hold of the message as their own and are now boldly proclaiming it.

Arriving at the verse in question, one should now have a better understanding of what it is saying. Let's look at the verse again: *"For all the Prophets and the Law prophesied until John" (Matthew 11:13).* After good exegetical work, one can conclusively state that this verse is not saying John the Baptist marked the end of prophecy. **Rather, it is referring to the fact that John is seeing the Kingdom unfold before his eyes. He is not just prophesying about it from afar, as one who longed for it. He is seeing up close, as one who is beholding it.**

If this is not enough evidence, we all know that John himself prophesied (John 1:27) about Jesus being among the people and greater than him. Furthermore, throughout Acts we have many prophecies. One is the prophecy about a great famine. *"And one of them named Agabus stood up and foretold by the Spirit that there would be a great famine over all the world (this took place in the days of Claudius)" (Acts 11:28).*

Prophecy did not end with John; he witnessed a new era. It was one that Joel prophesied in Joel 2 and Peter echoed in Acts 2.

"'And in the last days it shall be, God declares, that I will pour out my Spirit on all flesh, and your sons and your daughters shall prophesy, and your young men shall see visions, and your old men shall dream dreams…'" (Joel 2:28; Acts 2:17).

Prophecy cannot be dead. Jesus was the realization of Moses' desire that all were God's prophets, meaning they all had His Spirit and prophesied (spoke his word) (Numbers 11:29).

The Ministry of a Prophet

In the Old Testament there were schools that taught, possibly only a selected group of people, how to function as prophets. We see this exemplified in the prophet Samuel's life, as well as with Elijah and Elisha. First, let's look at the school that the prophet Samuel established.

When Saul was attempting to kill David, someone had told him that David was in Ramah at Naioth (1 Samuel 19:19). The word Naioth means "dwellings". It was here that many of the prophets and their sons lived. This has been viewed by some as a prophetic college.[1] It is at this place that Samuel trained many of his pupils on the prophetic ways (1 Samuel 19:18-24).

Samuel's training did not stop only with him. Elijah and Elisha also trained prophets. Elijah had a group of prophets who were very aware of who he was and although it does not mention it, one can get the sense that they were taught some things from Elijah. The statement by some of these prophets when they said to Elisha, *"...Do you know that today the LORD will take away your master from over you?" (2 Kings 2:3)* can suggest that Elisha was under the mentorship of Elijah because they called Elijah Elisha's master.

In response, Elisha did not make a statement indicating there was no relationship. In fact, based on the way Elisha pursued after Elijah from town to town, one can conclude that Elijah and Elisha were very close. Elisha, like Elijah mentored and trained prophets also. There are two specific prophets mentioned in the Bible who were close disciples of Elisha. The first one was Gehazi, who fell away for a time because of his greed (2 Kings 5:20-27). The second person who was being mentored closely by Elisha was someone whose name is never revealed. However, we do get to read a little about his interactions with Elisha in 2 Kings 6. He is known as Elisha's servant.

In the Old Testament, there seemed to have been great emphasis put on the prophetic. Prophets were trained and mentored. At times some were disciplined for their lack of discipline like Gehazi, when Elisha cursed him with Leprosy (2 Kings 5:20-27). All in all, the prophetic office was deeply revered. There is a lot one can learn about the prophetic ministry in the Old Testament that can help believers today navigate through the prophetic and understand the prophetic office.

Just like the apostles, the prophets work is also classified as foundational (Ephesians 2:18-20). Furthermore, the ministry of the prophet in the New Testament should not be too far removed from the Old Testament prophets. As the Old Testament prophets were the seers, and God spoke through them, so should the New Testament prophets be.

This doesn't mean they are carbon copies, though. We are in a new covenant now, whereas prophets of old had to abide by the law and an incorrect prophecy would get them stoned. In the New Testament, we get to experience a higher level of grace. This means prophesying wrong with the right heart will not get you stoned.

I'm not excusing false prophecy, but I am challenging the belief that a prophet must be perfect or perfectly hear God. **Even Samuel the prophet, could not discern the voice of God at first. He had to grow in God's Word so that he could discern God's voice (1 Samuel 3).**

In the New Testament in the book of Acts, there is a prophet who is mentioned as a prophet, Agabus. Agabus the prophet is mentioned both in Acts 11:27-30 and Acts 21:10-12. In Acts 11:27-30, Agabus *"...foretold by the Spirit that there would be a great famine over all the world (this took place in the days of Claudius)" (Acts 11:28).*

In response to the prophecy in Acts 11:27-30, we see the apostles sending Paul and Barnabas to deliver money and gifts to the Church in Judea in preparation for the famine. *"So the disciples determined, every one according to his ability, to send relief to the brothers living in Judea. And they did so, sending it to the elders by the hand of Barnabas and Saul" (Acts 11:29-30).*

There are a few things we can glean from this passage. One, the early church had prophets. Although Agabus is one of the only ones we truly get informed about by name, Luke clearly states there were multiple prophets. *"Now in these days prophets came down from Jerusalem to Antioch" (Acts 11:27).*

Secondly, the early church gave these prophets room to prophecy (Acts 11:28). Thirdly, the church not only heard the prophecy, but prayerfully acted on what was said. **Sometimes prophecy corresponds with how people respond.** In other words, the answer to the famine was not God stopping it, but the people acting in love towards those in need.

Lastly, what was prophesied came to pass and was noted as doing so (Acts 11:28). The reliability of the prophet is in part proven through the prophecy coming to pass or not. However, this is not the only true examination of a prophet. We will explore other ways to tell if a prophet is a false prophet or not in the next section.

The other place Agabus the prophet is mentioned is in Acts 21:10-12. I've covered this prophetic word extensively early in the GIFTS OF THE SPIRIT: MY SOUL. To recap, Paul was on his way to Rome when he ran into Agabus.

When he saw Paul, Agabus *"took Paul's belt and bound his own feet and hands and said, 'Thus says the Holy Spirit, 'This is how the Jews at Jerusalem will bind the man who owns this belt and deliver him into the hands of the Gentiles'"* (Acts 21:10-12).

When Agabus gave this prophetic word, it is obvious that his prophecies were revered. Those who heard the prophecy knew that it was going to happen so much so that they hardly relented from telling Paul to heed it. Paul did not say Agabus was a false prophet because what was said to him did not make him feel comfortable. Instead, he took it as a confirmation of what God had already spoken to him about.

In 1 Corinthians 14, Paul addresses the importance of prophecy, speaking in tongues and interpretation.

"Let two or three prophets speak, and let the others weigh what is said. If a revelation is made to another sitting there, let the first be silent. For you can all prophesy one by one, so that all may learn and all be encouraged, and the spirits of prophets are subject to prophets. For God is not a God of confusion but of peace. As in all the churches of the saints…" (1 Corinthians 14:29-33).

Notice yet again Paul is not speaking of prophets as if they are some foreign group of believers. He not only addresses them as prophets; he helps establish order as they are prophesying. Paul calls the prophecy "revelation", which means to reveal something that's hidden. In context, Paul is not simply saying these men are interpreting Scripture as some may say. Rather, they are revealing hidden things that God is showing.

Paul goes on to say that each prophet should take turns prophesying so that "all may learn and all be encouraged." Prophecy therefore is supposed to help us as believers to learn and encourage us to draw closer to God.

In no way is the prophet supposed to lose control. Some prophets prophesy out of turn and out of place because they are immature. Paul says, *"the spirits of prophets are subject to prophets" (1Corinthians 14:32).* "Subject to prophets" can be interpreted as "controlled by the prophet."

Here is an example of a prophet not controlling their prophetic gift. A friend of mine once told me a story about how when she was 16 years old, a prophet abused her through the words he spoke over her.

She was in a church service and this prophet was teaching. Someone made her laugh during service. The prophet got extremely irritated by her laughing and pointed at her and said, "may you never have children."

Now in her 40's when she was telling me this story, she broke down crying. She said, "Why would he say that to a teenager?" None of her relationships ever truly worked out and she's been in and out of the hospital and doctors have told her she may have cancer in her uterus.

There was no reason for this man to speak that over her. He could have controlled himself and used some of the fruit of the Spirit and patiently asked for everyone's attention. I also don't believe this was from God in any way. He actually cursed her instead of blessing her. **A prophecy can be detrimental when it's not in control.**

As we read this passage, in no way is Paul indicating one should not prophesy. Rather, he is encouraging it to be done as long as it's done in an orderly manner because *"God is not a God of confusion but of peace…" (1 Corinthians 14:33).* In our churches today, we don't even give room for the prophetic. Instead, we tend to silence the voice of God because of fears and insecurities. If we make room for prophets to prophesy, then God can make what's hidden plain.

False Prophets

Like all the other offices, the devil has a false replica. Jesus says,

"'Beware of false prophets, who come to you in sheep's clothing but inwardly are ravenous wolves. You will recognize them by their fruits. Are grapes gathered from thorn bushes, or figs from thistles? So, every healthy tree bears good fruit, but the diseased tree bears bad fruit. A healthy tree cannot bear bad fruit, nor can a diseased tree bear good fruit. Every tree that does not bear good fruit is cut down and thrown into the fire. Thus you will recognize them by their fruits…On that day

many will say to me, 'Lord, Lord, did we not prophesy in your name, and cast out demons in your name, and do many mighty works in your name?' And then will I declare to them, 'I never knew you; depart from me, you workers of lawlessness" (Matthew 7:15-23).

According to Jesus, the best way to tell if a prophet is false or not is by their fruit (Galatians 5:22-23). Many people believe a prophet is known by whether their prophecy comes true. This, however, is the smallest part of someone being a false prophet. Moses says,

"'If a prophet or a dreamer of dreams arises among you and gives you a sign or a wonder, and the sign or wonder that he tells you comes to pass, and if he says, 'Let us go after other gods,' which you have not known, 'and let us serve them,' you shall not listen to the words of that prophet or that dreamer of dreams. For the Lord your God is testing you, to know whether you love the Lord your God with all your heart and with all your soul'" (Deuteronomy 13:1-3).

Essentially, God is speaking through Moses and saying that some false prophets will prophecy correctly, and they may even do miracles and wonders. But ultimately this is to test our hearts to know whether we truly love God.

Before we go any further let us establish what a false prophet may look like. False prophets can be: witches, warlocks, medicine men, sorcerers, shamans, mediums, psychics, New Age teachers, the teachers of the occult, and teachers of any of the thousands of religions that do not believe Jesus is the only way to God and that He is the Son of God.

It is important for us as believers to distinguish the difference between a false prophet and a true prophet, especially since we are living in the last days (Matthew 24:11). When one rightly divides the Word of God in relation to prophets and prophecy, there is greater comprehension of a false prophet. According to the entirety of Scripture, false prophets will look and act like real prophets. It is vital for us as believers, therefore, to know our word, be able to identify the fruits of the Spirit, and not compromise on the Gospel of Jesus Christ!

CHAPTER 38

The Evangelist

Billy Graham witnessed to millions of people all around the world. He was, by definition, an evangelist. His central message was the power of the cross of Jesus Christ, and his longing was to see souls come to know the Lord.

On Goodreads.com one of the things Billy Graham is quoted that he said was, "God proved his love on the Cross. When Christ hung, and bled, and died, it was God saying to the world, 'I love you.'" **For an evangelist, the cross must be preached!**

After I won a $23,00 Dr. Pepper scholarship, another college student reached out to me because she too had entered the competition for the scholarship. She was hoping I could train her on how to throw the football (which was what determined how much money you won). I was living in New York at the time, and she was in Texas.

I rallied some friends of mine who were still in Texas and through video calls, I taught her my technique and gave her a few pointers. She ended up winning the competition, which was $100,000! After she won, on live television she gave praise to Jesus Christ and then, when asked about her technique, she talked about how I taught her the technique.

One day I decided to show this video of her praising Jesus to an evangelist I knew personally by the name of Dr. Scott Camp. I thought he would be amazed by the fact that she witnessed on live television. But to my astonishment, he was not impressed at all. In fact, he said, "You call that witnessing? She spoke more about you than Jesus."

I didn't even know how to feel. **Witnessing for an evangelist is more than just casually saying the name of Jesus. They want to see everyone repent and get saved.** I spent time with him and got to see and learn his perspective. It challenged me and made me more aware of the lost that are all around me every day.

I was so shaken inside hearing him share about eternity and the fact that millions even billions of people will one day not call heaven their home that I started witnessing to a lot more people. One day, while I was driving with a new-found heart for the lost, I saw someone walking and I stopped my car and asked him if he knew Jesus. He said he didn't, so I asked him if he wanted to know Jesus he said yes. I was able to lead him to the Lord.

Dr. Camp came to the town where I live for about a week and over 40 people got saved. The whole time he was in our town all he discussed was how we could win the whole town over to Christ. He had a passion for souls that I had not felt in a long time. This is why we need the evangelists in our congregation. They push us to reach out to our community, nation, and the world.

In the Bible, Paul commands Timothy to do the work of an evangelist (2 Timothy 4:5). What is an evangelist, and what is their role in the church body? How can we, like Timothy, learn from the evangelist?

Ministry of an Evangelist

The word evangelist means "messenger." The book of Acts has a great example of an evangelist in a man named Philip.

Philip the Evangelist enters the scene in Acts 6:5 after some Gentiles in the church are being neglected. The apostles had prayed for seven men to take care of the services in the church body, and he was one of the seven. Acts 6 makes it clear that the apostles were not the ones over these services, meaning Philip the Evangelist is different from Philip the brother of Andrew.

As we follow the life of Philip the Evangelist, we can glean from him what an evangelist is supposed to be doing. Not too long after we are introduced to Philip in Acts 6, persecution breaks out and Stephen becomes the first martyr. The believers, except for the apostles, all get scattered across Israel in Acts 8:1.

God doesn't waste trials, though. In His Sovereignty, God knew that through this persecution many would hear the good news (Acts 11:19). **Philip, being an evangelist, never allows a tragedy to be wasted; rather, he uses it as an opportunity to minister to the lost.** He did not just share the gospel with the Jews, but he even shared it with the Samaritans (Acts 8:5).

One particular story of his evangelistic work is found in Acts 8:26-40. After the believers were scattered, Philip was given an assignment by the Angel of the Lord.

"Now an angel of the Lord said to Philip, 'Rise and go toward the south to the road that goes down from Jerusalem to Gaza.' This is a desert place. And he rose and went. And there was an Ethiopian, a eunuch, a court official of Candace, queen of the Ethiopians, who was in charge of all her treasure. He had come to Jerusalem to worship and was returning, seated in his chariot, and he was reading the prophet Isaiah. And the Spirit said to Philip, 'Go over and join this chariot.' So

Philip ran to him and heard him reading Isaiah the prophet and asked, 'Do you understand what you are reading?' And he said, 'How can I, unless someone guides me?' And he invited Philip to come up and sit with him. Now the passage of the Scripture that he was reading was this:

'Like a sheep he was led to the slaughter
and like a lamb before its shearer is silent,
so he opens not his mouth.
In his humiliation justice was denied him.
Who can describe his generation?
For his life is taken away from the earth.'

And the eunuch said to Philip, 'About whom, I ask you, does the prophet say this, about himself or about someone else?' Then Philip opened his mouth and beginning with this Scripture he told him the good news about Jesus. And as they were going along the road they came to some water, and the eunuch said, 'See, here is water! What prevents me from being baptized?' And he commanded the chariot to stop, and they both went down into the water, Philip and the eunuch, and he baptized him. And when they came up out of the water, the Spirit of the Lord carried Philip away, and the eunuch saw him no more, and went on his way rejoicing. But Philip found himself at Azotus, and as he passed through he preached the gospel to all the towns until he came to Caesarea."

There is so much in this passage that someone could write a book specifically on this passage. Let's look at each verse and decrypt it. The passage starts out with Philip getting an assignment from the Angel of the Lord. The Angel tells him to go to "the road that goes down from Jerusalem to Gaza." This is a desert place (Acts 8:26).

As he gets to this place, he sees a caravan carrying a Eunuch of the Queen of Ethiopia. The Spirit of God tells him to go near the caravan. It's important to note that for an evangelist, it does not matter what your social, economic, gender, race, status is. For them, sharing the Gospel has to do with being obedient to God.

As he approaches the caravan, he overhears the Eunuch reading Isaiah 53, the Messianic passage. Unable to discern what he's reading; the eunuch asks Philip who the writer is talking about. Philip, being at the right place at the right time, tells him about Jesus.

After talking to him about Jesus, notice what Philip doesn't do. He doesn't say well you have to go through 12 weeks of courses before you can get baptized. Or you better sign up with the non-denominational church or else you won't make it.

The Holy Spirit even took him before he had a chance to teach this Eunuch more about Christ. Here lies one of the differences between an evangelist and the other offices. An evangelist is called to share the message spread the seed to whoever is willing to hear. They may go to places, share the gospel, and never return to those places ever again. It is the pastor's job to shepherd the people, as we'll look at later. This shows that the job of an evangelist does not necessarily focus on discipleship; his or her job is to win souls.

The eunuch asks to be baptized after Philip shares the Gospel of Jesus Christ with him and Philip obliges. They didn't wait for some special occasion; they just did it. Afterward, the Holy Spirit took Philip. He literally caused Philip to disappear and reappear somewhere else.

Evangelists don't necessarily like staying inside the church building, nor is that their job. Their main role is to win souls and help the church grow. **They may get irritated when the community around them is being neglected. Empty chairs, to them, means there is room for more people to come hear the good news.**

False Evangelists

Both the Mormon Church and Jehovah's Witnesses send their congregates to evangelize. They come and speak to you about Jesus, but inside they don't truly know Him. Paul states,

"But even if we or an angel from heaven should preach to you a gospel contrary to the one we preached to you, let him be accursed. As we have said before, so now I say again: If anyone is preaching to you a gospel contrary to the one you received, let him be accursed" (Galatians 1:8-9).

Knowing the gospel, therefore, is essential in detecting false evangelism. And what is the Gospel of Jesus Christ? In Ephesians 2, Paul gives a great definition of the gospel. He starts out by explaining that we all were sinners (Ephesians 2:1-4).

The first thing to understand about the gospel is that to receive it, we must believe we need it. Understanding you're a sinner in need of a savior helps open the door for the gospel. This means anyone who evangelizes to you contrary to this truth is a false evangelist.

Secondly, understand what God did for you. You needed saving, so God because He is merciful and He loves you, showed you love by sending His Son Jesus Christ to die for you on the cross while you were still a sinner. It is by His grace you receive salvation (Ephesians 2:4-6; Romans 5:8). Therefore, if anyone states there is more than one way to God and that it's Jesus plus Joseph Smith, that you are saved by only being in a certain community, or that you must work to earn your salvation, they are preaching a different gospel and falsely evangelizing to you.

Thirdly, you must know who you are in Jesus Christ. Jesus did not stay dead; He rose up from the grave. In so doing, you also rose up with Him. He, being the Son of God, made you also the Son of God, and being now seated with Christ, He made you seated with Him also. His authority is your authority. You're no longer dead, but alive in Him by placing your trust in Him (Ephesians 2:7-9).

Lastly, you *"are his workmanship, created in Christ Jesus for good works, which God prepared beforehand, that we should walk in them" (Ephesians 2:8).* You are no longer a slave to sin. Some have falsely stated, "we fellowship in our sin." We do not fellowship in our sin; rather our fellowship is with Him. Our lives now demonstrate the glory of God to the world. We are His prized possession.

Anyone who comes to you and tries to evangelize to you using another Gospel is a false evangelist. When I say this, I'm not referring to someone who mistakenly says the wrong thing with a right heart toward God. Intentionality, when exposed, reveals a person's mentality, which reveals their reality. In other words, a person's motives reveal their character.

Paul states this about the one who falsifies the Gospel.

"I am astonished that you are so quickly deserting him who called you in the grace of Christ and are turning to a different gospel— not that there is another one, but there are some who trouble you and want to distort the gospel of Christ. But even if we or an angel from heaven should preach to you a gospel contrary to the one we preached to you, let him be accursed. As we have said before, so now I say again: If anyone is preaching to you a gospel contrary to the one you received, let him be accursed" (Galatians 1:6-9).

The word *accursed* means "set for destruction", or in this context, "separated from Christ." In today's church, how many people have perverted the gospel and preached something that's not the true gospel? We must be careful how we share the gospel and what we share as gospel.

CHAPTER 39

The Pastor

My father-in-law, Rick Winkowitsch, is a farmer in Cut Bank, Montana. He used to own 200+ sheep. Through his interactions with the sheep, he has learned a great deal on what it means to be a shepherd. There is hardly a time when he speaks about a church that he does not draw attention to the similarities between sheep and people and a shepherd and a pastor.

He would often talk about the importance of a shepherd knowing his sheep. For him, the sheep must recognize the shepherd's voice. **When the shepherd calls, the sheep should know how to respond to his calling.** At times, their ability to respond can save their lives.

He would mention how helpless the sheep are. He shared with us how sheep can die from: getting stuck on their back, too much food, drowning, attacked by flies, eaten by maggots, being attacked by any creature, being frightened (they can have a heart attack), suffocating in snow, being too cold, being too hot, etc.

Yet this is only the tip of the iceberg for sheep. My father-in-law once told me that there are certain sheep who will be rebellious. If they are not taken care of quickly by the shepherd, they will cause the whole flock to be led astray.

The rebellious sheep are sometimes fat and when there is feed, they push the other sheep out of the way. They are never content and are always looking for greener pastures. Once they find a way out of the fenced area, they will always escape or try to escape through that area. The rest of the sheep will unfortunately follow the ungrateful sheep, infecting the whole flock with ungratefulness.

These rebellious sheep can also be gluttonous and greedy. He has seen some rebellious sheep eat oats so fast they died. The shepherd must therefore be vigilant, always watching. If sheep don't have good boundaries established, they can get lost and influenced wrongly.

These comparisons are very important when viewed through the lens of Scripture. The Bible refers to us as sheep. Jesus says when speaking about those who are his, *"My sheep hear my voice, and I know them, and they follow me" (John 10:27).*

The Scripture also calls Christ "the good shepherd" (John 10:14). He knows those who are His and He does them no harm. He gives them life eternal and feeds and cleanses them with His Word. He does not force His sheep; He persuades them to pursue Him.

Ministry of a Pastor

The word pastor in Greek is *poimen*, meaning "shepherd." The pastor, as well as all the other offices, are called to oversee the flock. The difference though, between how the other offices oversee and how a pastor is called to oversee, is in their God-given assignments. The word for overseer, elder, or bishop is *episkopos* in the Greek.

The connotation of the Greek word *apostolos* sometimes had to do with one who went before the emperor came and led a military fleet by ship to a new land to conquer it. They would be the representative of the one who sent them. The term *episkopos,* in the Greek culture, had to do with someone who, after the Romans conquered a city, is established as a commissioner over that particular city or state.[1]

They would answer to the emperor. Since the emperor could not be there himself, he would send "apostolos", messengers, to the episkopos to relay his message. Sometimes, this message contained guidance for their conquest. The one who was being sent by the king had the authority of the king. In Hebrew, this is represented by the word *shaliah*. This term focused more on the commissioning aspect of the one being sent. Consequently, the messenger was empowered by the sender and was sent on an envoy with their authority.[2]

Although the Kingdom of God is not merely bound by these definitions, one can see the correlations through the semantics that help us to get a better understanding of the author's reasoning. Furthermore, what the Holy Spirit was expressing to them can be better understood, helping us comprehend what the Word of God is projecting to us today.

Considering this, what then is the ministry of the pastor? **Number one, the pastor's job is not to *be* the emperor, but to extend the emperor's reign.** This is done by representing him and making sure what the emperor wants to happen and how he wants it to happen is adhered to. The laws that are established will not be foreign but in direct relation with the desires of the emperor.

This is where the terms change. In the worldly concept, the episkopos should rule with total authority. Yet the Bible warns against being domineering. It is an abuse of power. Peter says this as it relates to elders,

"'So I exhort the elders among you, as a fellow elder and a witness of the sufferings of Christ, as well as a partaker in the glory that is going to be revealed: shepherd the flock of God that is among you, exercising oversight, not under compulsion, but willingly, as God would have you; not for shameful gain, but eagerly; not domineering over those in your charge, but being examples to the flock. And when the chief Shepherd appears, you will receive the unfading crown of glory" (1 Peter 5:1-4).

Within this passage we get a pretty clear picture of what God expects from a pastor. First, they must shepherd the flock of God overseeing them. As I previously illustrated through my father-in-law, a shepherd must know his sheep. They must guard them from wolves and lead them to the right pasture.

This means the pastor must preach the Word and check on the people, making sure they are feeding themselves the right food and not being led astray by every doctrine of men. Peter goes on to say, *"not under compulsion, but willingly, as God would have you" (1 Peter 5:2).* The heart in which you shepherd affects the people you are shepherding. To be under compulsion is to forcefully act on something. **When one must force themselves to serve the Lord, the heart of the gospel is lost.**

It should never be that I *have* to pastor; it should be I *get* to pastor. It is out of this heart that there is genuine health. When Peter says "willingly", he doesn't mean as *you* will it but as *God* wills it. It's connected to the next phrase, "as God would have you", meaning as God wills it.

Peter goes on to say, *"not for shameful gain, but eagerly…" (1 Peter 5:2).* Shepherds must be careful not to be led or be motivated by a paycheck or their accolades. There should be a genuine joy for the things of God.

Next, the passage goes on to say, *"not domineering over those in your charge, but being examples to the flock" (1 Peter 5:3).* To unpack the word domineering, I believe the synonyms for it help bring the best clarity to its meaning: "browbeat, bully, intimidate, push around/about, order about/around, lord it over; dictate to, be overbearing, have under one's thumb, rule with a rod of iron; informal boss about/around, walk all over.[3]

Many pastors see their flocks as their subjects, which in turn makes the people mere objects instead of people God died for. When we lord it over people, we strip people of their God-given authority and put ourselves in the place of God in their life. This in turn causes the gospel to be maligned by the world because church becomes based on man's standards instead of Christ's revelation of the gospel.

But the pastor who leads by example is indeed like Christ. Christ emptied himself of his divinity and endured death on the cross (Philippians 2). He does not force people to follow Him; He challenges and loves them where they are. He gently leads us and is never domineering.

Pastors must remember that they are the substitutes and that God is the true shepherd. As Peter writes, *"And when the Chief Shepherd appears, you will receive the unfading crown of glory" (1 Peter 5:4).* If pastors insist on being domineering, they steal God's glory here on earth, and miss out on heavens unfading glory.

False Shepherds

As he was departing the church in Ephesus, Paul addresses the elders and says,

"Pay careful attention to yourselves and to all the flock, in which the Holy Spirit has made you overseers, to care for the church of God, which he obtained with his own blood. I know that after my departure fierce wolves will come in among you, not sparing the flock; and from among your own selves will arise men speaking twisted things, to draw away the disciples after them. Therefore be alert, remembering that for three years I did not cease night or day to admonish every one with tears." (Acts 20:28)

Paul, who knows his time here on earth is running out, says the most important things he could say to the church in Ephesus as he is about to leave. He warns them by prophesying to them what's to come. He starts out by telling them to pay close attention to themselves and the flock.

His reasoning is that after his departure, fierce wolves will come. He warns them of two ways they will come. One way is from the outside and the other is from the inside. The wolves from the outside will not spare the flock, as it seems that they are bent on destruction.

The ones from the inside will twist true teaching and lead some disciples astray. Usually, their tactic is deception. What's shocking is that Paul says these will rise up from among you, meaning there were some in their midst whose hearts were not truly devoted to Christ.

We, like the church in Ephesus, must be on guard. Overseers must be careful what they allow into the church. Not every speaker is sent from God; the devil also has his ministers who masquerade themselves as ministers of light (2 Corinthians 11:13-15).

We need to also be cautious of those inside the church who focus more on *"...myths and endless genealogies, which promote speculations rather than the stewardship from God that is by faith" (1 Timothy 1:4).* **Good questions to ask are: What does this have to do with the gospel? How do people come to the gospel through this? How does this cause the gospel to advance?**

When speaking to Ezekiel, God made a sharp warning against false shepherds. This warning, although written first to Israel, is applicable to us today. As you read Ezekiel 34, honestly assess what a true shepherd should look like.

"The word of the Lord came to me: 'Son of man, prophesy against the shepherds of Israel; prophesy, and say to them, even to the shepherds, Thus says the Lord God: Ah, shepherds of Israel who have been feeding yourselves! Should not shepherds feed the sheep? You eat the fat, you clothe yourselves with the wool, you slaughter the fat ones, but you do not feed the sheep. The weak you have not strengthened, the sick you have not healed, the injured you have not bound up, the strayed you have not brought back, the lost you have not sought, and with force and harshness you have ruled them. So they were scattered, because there was no shepherd, and they became food for all the wild beasts. My sheep were scattered; they wandered over all the mountains and on every high hill. My sheep

were scattered over all the face of the earth, with none to search or seek for them.

'Therefore, you shepherds, hear the word of the Lord: As I live, declares the Lord God, surely because my sheep have become a prey, and my sheep have become food for all the wild beasts, since there was no shepherd, and because my shepherds have not searched for my sheep, but the shepherds have fed themselves, and have not fed my sheep, therefore, you shepherds, hear the word of the Lord: Thus says the Lord God, Behold, I am against the shepherds, and I will require my sheep at their hand and put a stop to their feeding the sheep. No longer shall the shepherds feed themselves. I will rescue my sheep from their mouths, that they may not be food for them.'

The Lord God Will Seek Them Out

'For thus says the Lord God: Behold, I, I myself will search for my sheep and will seek them out. As a shepherd seeks out his flock when he is among his sheep that have been scattered, so will I seek out my sheep, and I will rescue them from all places where they have been scattered on a day of clouds and thick darkness. And I will bring them out from the peoples and gather them from the countries, and will bring them into their own land. And I will feed them on the mountains of Israel, by the ravines, and in all the inhabited places of the country. I will feed them with good pasture, and on the mountain heights of Israel shall be their grazing land. There they shall lie down in good grazing land, and on rich pasture they shall feed on the mountains of Israel. I myself will be the shepherd of my sheep, and I myself will

make them lie down, declares the Lord God. I will seek the lost, and I will bring back the strayed, and I will bind up the injured, and I will strengthen the weak, and the fat and the strong I will destroy. I will feed them in justice.

'As for you, my flock, thus says the Lord God: Behold, I judge between sheep and sheep, between rams and male goats. Is it not enough for you to feed on the good pasture, that you must tread down with your feet the rest of your pasture; and to drink of clear water, that you must muddy the rest of the water with your feet? And must my sheep eat what you have trodden with your feet, and drink what you have muddied with your feet?

'Therefore, thus says the Lord God to them: Behold, I, I myself will judge between the fat sheep and the lean sheep. Because you push with side and shoulder, and thrust at all the weak with your horns, till you have scattered them abroad, I will rescue my flock; they shall no longer be a prey. And I will judge between sheep and sheep. And I will set up over them one shepherd, my servant David, and he shall feed them: he shall feed them and be their shepherd. And I, the Lord, will be their God, and my servant David shall be prince among them. I am the Lord; I have spoken.

The Lord's Covenant of Peace
'I will make with them a covenant of peace and banish wild beasts from the land, so that they may dwell securely in the wilderness and sleep in the woods. And I will

make them and the places all around my hill a blessing, and I will send down the showers in their season; they shall be showers of blessing. And the trees of the field shall yield their fruit, and the earth shall yield its increase, and they shall be secure in their land. And they shall know that I am the Lord, when I break the bars of their yoke, and deliver them from the hand of those who enslaved them. They shall no more be a prey to the nations, nor shall the beasts of the land devour them. They shall dwell securely, and none shall make them afraid. And I will provide for them renowned plantations so that they shall no more be consumed with hunger in the land, and no longer suffer the reproach of the nations. And they shall know that I am the Lord their God with them, and that they, the house of Israel, are my people, declares the Lord God. And you are my sheep, human sheep of my pasture, and I am your God, declares the Lord God.'"

CHAPTER 40

The Teacher

The teacher may be last on this list, but it in no way are they the least. For instance, let's look at what teachers have helped do for our society, before schools became the government's way of indoctrination.

There was a time when schools were places that celebrated truth. Not many people know this, but most of our Ivy League schools such as Harvard, Yale, Princeton were all started by ministers of the gospel with the intended purpose of serving the gospel.

When these great men decided to start these schools, truth was of the utmost importance. They knew that unless people were taught truth, our society could no longer recognize the gospel. **Preachers preached, but teachers taught how to preach.**

Although the pursuit of truth in the school system has dwindled and opinionated theories have sought to brainwash our communities, there are still plenty of teachers who are willing to risk it all for the sake of truth. It is these teachers who help reach not just the minds of the students but help shape their hearts.

These teachers help students not just get their way but truly know the way. Through rational thought and reliance on truth only, they teach students how to truly think critically. **Their disposition is not based on biased bigotry set on them by the government; rather, it's on the need to know and teach the truth.** Teachers must teach that emotional responses, although necessary at times, does not necessarily equate to truth.

One can't just simply feel like they are right. Feelings must line up with knowledge. **Subsequently, if we live in a society where relativity is taught, then truth is elusive, leading many to see truth as abusive instead of our ally in a world full of lies.**

Therefore, a teacher's role is extremely important. It's imperative that teachers do not present their opinions, but present truth and let those listening think rationally about what they're hearing. No one is perfect, so at times biases will arise. However, it is up to the teacher to address the biases and give those learning opportunities to factually concede or relent from the statements made by the teacher.

The Teacher's Ministry

One of the names Jesus was called repeatedly was *Rabbi*, which means "teacher" in Hebrew. When He was here on earth, Jesus taught prolifically. From the Sermon on the Mount to the ascension to Heaven, Jesus never let a moment pass without teaching the truth. He would teach in many ways using items people knew about, historical events, parables, and anything He saw fit into the narrative of the teachings.

After Jesus ascended, He sent us the Holy Spirit to continue teaching us. It's the Holy Spirit's job to reveal Jesus to us and lead us all to truth (John 14). The Holy Spirit is our first teacher. John expounds on this concept when he writes,

"But you have received the Holy Spirit, and he lives within you, so you don't need anyone to teach you what is true. For the Spirit teaches you everything you need to know, and what he teaches is true--it is not a lie. So just as he has taught you, remain in fellowship with Christ" (1 John 2:27 NLT).

John in no way is saying get rid of our earthly teachers. If this were true, there would be no need for us to follow what he wrote. Rather, he is making sure all those learning, discern what is taught through the Holy Spirit only. As believers, we don't truly need earthly teachers like we don't need apostles, prophets, evangelists, and pastors. We must submit to their leadership, though, because they are interwoven into God's plan of redemption.

Since Scripture prescribes them as necessary in accomplishing growth and guarding us from wolves, we therefore must heed them. Our alliance is not with men it's with God, and with whatever means He deems necessary to advancing his purpose. When we submit to these leaders, we are not doing it to please them but to obey God.

A great example of this would be Christians who are in a foreign country that does not allow the Word of God into the country. Though these people don't have the Word, they still know the truth of the word. Indeed, it is the Spirit of God who reveals the depth of God's heart (1 Corinthians 2:10). If you know the Holy Spirit, you know God.

Therefore, the first thing a teacher of God's Word should have is the Spirit of God. It can be said, **before the disciples truly taught, the Spirit they surely sought, before they gave what they knew, He made their hearts brand new.** Anyone aspiring to be a teacher must fall in love with the greatest Teacher here on earth, the Holy Spirit.

The second thing all teachers must have is a knowledge of the gospel embedded in their hearts. Without the knowledge of the gospel, a man's heart remains hostile. A teacher must know and teach the right gospel (Galatians 1).

False teachers arise when people make the gospel secondary instead of their primary prize. What then is the gospel? Jesus Christ is the gospel; all He was, is, and will be. It's the good news! It's the foundation of our faith.

Through the gospel, one can truly understand salvation. We receive what we did not initiate, but it was Jesus who first loved us. It had nothing to do with our goodness, but His God-ness.

If teachers don't know the gospel, they will make Pharisees and not disciples. It's easy for someone who teaches to get religious because the enticing part of information is it can cause one to believe it is transformation. Yet knowledge puffs up, and love builds up (1 Corinthians 8:1). We need knowledge, but we shouldn't assume that learning about God makes people have a yearning for God.

Thirdly, someone who sits in the office of a teacher must know the Word of God. We tend to have many fallacies and it can be easy for us to gravitate towards falsehood. God's Word helps safeguard us from being led astray and leading others astray.

Since people follow those they are learning from, a teacher of the Word should meditate on it day and night so that they are ready in and out of season (2 Timothy 4:2). It is from this foundation that those who teach will rightly divide truth. When Paul says to

Titus, *"But as for you, teach what accords with sound doctrine" (Titus 2:1)*, he does not mean teach men's traditions. He is imploring Titus to teach what lines up with the Word.

There are many more things about the ministry of a teacher that are vital, but these three things I believe are core: The Holy Spirit, the gospel, and the Word of God. All these things, anchored on Christ, are of the utmost importance for anyone aspiring to sit in the office of a teacher.

False Teachers

Unfortunately, the church has become no different than the world in many ways. The Bible says,

"For the time is coming when people will not endure sound teaching, but having itching ears they will accumulate for themselves teachers to suit their own passions, and will turn away from listening to the truth and wander off into myths" (2 Timothy 4:3-4).

The word for "sound" here is the word *hugiainó* (hoog-ee-ah'-ee-no). It means "wellness, safe, wholesome, uncorrupted."[1]

Here, Paul is telling Timothy that there will arise a time when people will no longer heed safe uncorrupted truth. Instead, they will, based on their desires, find teachers who are inclined to teach what they want to hear as an alternative to truth and pursue myths or ungodly opinions.

We right now are living in the time that Paul warned about. Therefore, I believe a teacher's role in the church is vital. If we do not teach sound doctrine in our churches, we will slowly fall into complacency. We are already seeing the effects of false teachers all around us.

Issues that have been very clear in Scripture are now being treated as if those writing the Scriptures were misled on those matters. One example is homosexuality. Currently, some denominations are publicly split on this matter. Even in the small town I lived in, there is was a church that split because of this issue.

How does this happen? How can something that the Word of God speaks very clearly about become lost in translation? Did the Word of God change? No!

The answer, again, is found in what Paul says, *"For the time is coming when people will not endure sound teaching, but having itching ears they will accumulate for themselves teachers to suit their own passions...".*

There are two things in this passage that stick out to me. One is the word "endure". This is the same word for endurance or perseverance. The Bible repeatedly speaks on the importance of having endurance. In speaking about the end times, Jesus says, *"But the one who endures to the end will be saved" (Matthew 24:13).*

When you must endure something, it means that thing is not easy. **Enduring truth is not easy because truth reveals lies and commands change.** A true teacher, though, must continue to speak the truth even though people may shun them. Only the truth can set people free!

The second thing that stands out to me is the phrase "suit their own passions." This refers to people viewing the truth as being relative. Truth cannot be based merely on how a person feels or his or her perception of the world. Truth cannot yield to us; we must yield to it.

As teachers of the gospel, we must be cautious. One cannot surrender truth because someone's feelings might get hurt. Teachers must remember in the last days, God has called people to persevere. This means it may be painful at times, but the higher vision is that people would know and be set free by the truth.

CHAPTER 41

Conclusion: Meeting Jesus in my Dream

Continuous immaturity is an issue in our churches. It is therefore very important for us as believers to do all that we can do in God's power to mature. **The system that man has established for the churches is not producing many mature believers.**

We should not be okay with people saying they are Christians and living worse than the world. I've found that many Christians don't truly know the gospel, so they live a very nominal life. But Jesus is coming back for a spotless bride (2 Corinthians 11:2; Ephesians 5:27).

We have a responsibility to accurately represent God and His Word. God is going to shake up all that is man-made until only what He has established will remain (Hebrews 12:26-28). God's kingdom is all that will remain.

Therefore, let us only seek to establish what is lined up with His kingdom. We cannot stay children in the faith. Things must be put back into order in the house of God. Grow up, church!!

The Hebrew writer I believe is speaking right to this situation when he says,

"About this we have much to say, and it is hard to explain, since you have become dull of hearing. For though by this time you ought to be teachers, you need someone to teach you again the basic principles of the oracles of God. You need milk, not solid food, for everyone who lives on milk is unskilled in the word of righteousness, since he is a child. But solid food is for the mature, for those who

have their powers of discernment trained by constant practice to distinguish good

from evil" (Hebrews 5:11-14 ESV).

This, I believe, represents where we are in our churches today. We're living off milk, unskilled in the Word of righteousness. My heart, though, is for the church to be at a place where we can eat solid food. It takes consistent practice. **We must train to be a Christian instead of trying to be a Christian.**

My Dream About Jesus

From as far back as I can remember, I had always wanted to die. Even after I got saved, I still would continually want to die. The only thing that changed was the way I asked God to die. Instead of saying I wish "I was dead", I started asking God to take me to Heaven because it sounded "holier."

My wife, who I was courting at the time, told me that these were Christian suicidal thoughts. I was perplexed by what she said, but something in me knew she was right. But even this did not stop me from asking God to take me.

One day, I ran into a prophet who looked at me and said, "You've had a Spirit of death chasing you your whole life." I looked at him, stunned. *How did he know this about me?* Still, even after this encounter, I would still go to my prayer room and beg God to take me.

Not long after the encounter with the prophet, I had a dream that I went to Heaven. In this dream, I encountered Jesus and saw Him in his humanity, full of humility. It was glorious! As I slept, I dreamt I went to Heaven, but it looked like the earth. As soon as I arrived, I heard kids around me go "we want to go see David" but I said, "I want to go see Jesus."

As I looked to my right, I saw what resembled a building made of glass with black metal brackets around the glass. It was about two stories high and the glass was tinted dark. When I first saw Jesus, He looked exactly like the painting the young artist Akiana painted of Him, but I didn't know about the painting until after the dream.

After I saw his face, Jesus knew I wanted to wash His feet. Suddenly, there was a bucket with water and a chair where Jesus sat. His feet were bare and dirty. I stared at Him, smiling from ear to ear, and began to scrub His feet. His big toe had some green goo under it, but I didn't care. I was going to scrub it all.

All of a sudden, He got up and went to go play with some kids. He was smiling and full of joy. Then He asked, "Where did I put that tool?" I thought, *why is he asking a question? Isn't He God?* Within seconds after this thought went through my mind, it felt as if my mind and His mind became one. It was like our minds went into hyperdrive. I could see that He had super knowledge, and my brain felt like it became the internet moving rapidly through information. It was going into light speed, like the Star Wars ship, until Jesus said, "There it is." One hundred percent God and one hundred percent man.

After this I saw Jesus' face. He was very sorrowful. It reminded me of the scene from *Passion of Christ* when Jesus got beat so bad that His eye swelled up. That's how He looked as He looked through a glass down at the world.

He then approached me and came to where I was, about an arm's length away. He said, "Do you want to go back?" I stared at Him and said nothing. He continued,

"Because there are still some more things, you're supposed to add to in the end times." As soon as He said end times, I saw the earth, globe-sized, above His head. It had two storm clouds.

One was going from NW to SE around the globe while the other was going NE to SW and around the globe. In the center they made an X as they crossed each other. Covering them was lightning and thunder and fire, and they were spinning as they were going. **I saw the end of the world.**

I still said nothing to Jesus. He leaned down closer to me and smiled, eyes full of joy. He said, "I'll come visit you in your dreams." I still did not respond. After this, He went on His way. I watched him as he went to pack another person's bag that was going back to earth through what looked like an elevator.

The beauty of it all was knowing that Jesus is number one in humility and He was going to remain number one for eternity. It melted my heart. He was serving everyone. They all knew He was Jesus, but he was so meek that everyone had a place.

As I observed him packing the bags, I decided I would go back. I grabbed my backpack, which happened to be next to me, threw it on with my right hand, and got up. As soon as I got up, I woke up in real life. I was full of blissful euphoria. At that moment, I knew the desire to die was broken off of me.

But what did it all mean? The Holy Spirit revealed to me that in the beginning of the dream, I showed up to a place that was Heaven, yet it looked like earth. This was because we are supposed to pray that Heaven would invade earth (Matthew 6:9-13)!

When I saw Jesus, He knew I wanted to wash His feet, so He sat down on the chair and His feet were dirty. Jesus' body is the church, and when we serve the church, we serve Jesus. The sorrowful look had to do with the pain He feels because people are headed to hell if they don't turn to Him.

His statement, "There's still some more things you're supposed to add to in the end times" has to do with souls. We cannot take anything to Heaven with us except for our neighbor. The earth was on fire because we are living in the last days.

It's amazing to me that a statement like "I want to go to heaven" can be hijacked by the devil. Deception can sound like truth. It was my encounter with Jesus that changed my path and broke the spirit of death off my life.

God has called us to advance His kingdom here on earth. He has given us all the tools necessary to accomplish it (2 Peter 1:3). We must mature in our thinking and our actions will follow.

Tests

My suggestion before you take these tests is that you pray and fast. I would personally recommend taking 1-3 days, depending on the leading of the Holy Spirit. Try to avoid answering "sometimes" unless it's truly necessary.

Understand that this test is meant to point you in the right direction, but it's not inerrant. If you get answers that are the same ask yourself this question: *Which one of these personalities did I have to grow in and which one has always been a part of me since I was young?*

THE PERSONALITY GIFTS: MY SPIRIT

1 Never me **2** Almost never me **3** Sometimes me **4** Almost always me **5** Always me

A.

1. I love to communicate and enforce revealed truth ___

2. I see things black or white; no gray areas ___

3. If someone is sinning it's easy for me to tell them the truth ___

4. Telling someone the truth is showing them mercy ___

5. Everything you say should always be founded in truth ___

B.

1. I love waiting tables and picking up after people; it gives me a sense of joy ___

2. I believe everyone should be working for Jesus at all times ___

3. Mark 10:45 "For the Son of man came not to be served but to serve, and to give his life as a ransom for many." This is one of my favorite verses. ___

4. If a man of God came into my house. I believe it's more important to serve him than to just sit and listen to him. ___

5. If I'm not working, I feel like I'm not productive and I'm being lazy ___

C.

1. Information leads to transformation ___

2. When I share a message I like to include dates and places ___

3. Nothing brings me more joy than someone learning how to think ___

4. There's always freedom in getting an education ___

5. I take pride in what I've learned ___

D.

1. I believe God is not angry ___

2. When someone sins, it's of the utmost importance that we love them ___

3. People make mistakes because they don't know any better ___

4. All people need is someone to believe in them ___

5. I love sending people uplifting words anonymously ___

E.

1. I don't want anyone to ever know when I give them something ___

2. I like knowing where my gift that I give is going ___

3. Once I give someone something i never ask for it back or bring it up again___

4. I don't expect a thank you after I give someone something ___

5. I was never taught how to share I just do it because it brings me joy ___

F.

1. Passion is one of the most important attributes; without it we die ___

2. I'm good at delegating work ___

3. My ceiling is other people's foundation. I want people to do greater things than me ___

4. I love the responsibility that comes with being a captain of a team ___

5. I always figure out a way to get a project done and to get people involved in accomplishing it ___

G.

1. It's hard for me to discipline anyone or to watch someone being disciplined ___

2. I believe love is always more needed than truth ___

3. We must always love people out of their sin ___

4. If I had to choose between love and truth in a situation, I would always choose love ___

5. I feel like we should always be gracious to someone ___

H.

1. I love to entertain people in my house ___

2. I've always wanted an extra bedroom or house to put someone in who needed a place to stay ___

3. I don't have to know you to welcome you into my house ___

4. When a stranger comes into my house, I'm ok with them using the best things in my house ___

5. I always wish I could house all the homeless people ___

A. Prophecy _____

B. Service _____

C. Teacher _____

D. Encourager _____

E. Giver _____

F. Leader _____

G. Mercy Shower _____

H. Hospitality _____

TEST on The Gifts of Operation: My Soul

1 Never me **2** Almost never me **3** Sometimes me **4** Almost always me **5** Always me

Oral Gifts

   A.

   1. I often find myself giving messages in tongues _____

   2. For me, service should always make room for a message in tongues _____

   3. A church that gives place for a message of tongues is a church that makes room for God to move _____

   4. If I go to another country that doesn't speak my language, God can supernaturally speak through me in their language_____

   5. I look forward to God teaching me new tongues _____

   B.

   1. When someone speaks in tongues, I almost always know what is being said _____

   2. I've been used often to interpret a message in tongues _____

   3. I have to find out what I'm saying when I speak in tongues _____

   4. I have distinguished when someone was speaking angelic tongues, mysterious tongues, and someone speaking a foreign language in tongues _____

   5. I have been used by God or have wanted to be used to translate someone who was speaking in tongues _____

C.

1. More often than not I can tell what's coming ahead for individuals or within situations _____

2. I constantly get dreams or words for people that either has to do with their present situation or what's to come for them _____

3. I store up prophetic words because I believe they are a weapon that can be used against the enemy _____

4. Whenever I go to an event I almost always can sense what's going to take place next _____

5. Countless times I've dreamt things that happened and spoken things that happened _____

Knowing Gifts

D.

1. I can consistently tell what happened in someone's past and what happened in past situations _____

2. Gods given me names of people, places they lived, schools they went too, and parents they had all before they told me or I've felt as if I should know this about people _____

3. I find myself on a regular basis telling people what they are going through or have gone through without them telling me _____

4. I find myself getting supernatural insight on how to finish or start projects that I had no education for _____

5. Truth is revealed to me about past or present situations on a regular basis

E.

1. I often have supernatural insight for what someone should do In a situation_____

2. I often feel like God is using me to share Information with the body on how we should proceed so our church will become more healthy_____

3. I often feel God prompting me to give wise instruction or advice to people when they need help_____

4. Heeding biblical wisdom and instruction such as Proverbs is paramount to having a healthy and thriving Church_____

5. I often ask the question in the church and of individuals "is this action/decision wise?"_____

F.

1. When I meet someone I can often tell the spirit that is influencing them._____

2. Whenever someone is talking I can often tell their true motives behind what they say._____

3. I can usually tell when and how people are being deceived_____

4. When I see so much deception in the church it motivates me to study the truth of the Bible so that I can know how to correct it_____

5. I don't trust people easily because the heart of man is exceedingly wicked_____

Power Gifts

G.

1. I always feel persuaded by God to do things _____

2. God has placed an innate ability for me to trust him, it is nearly impossible for me not to _____

3. I believe God can do anything in His word so I rely on him for everything _____

4. It's hard for me to see evil in a person because I know God can save them _____

5. I feel that God has caused me to always be confident in Him since I've been saved. I can't hardly remember a time that I was not confident that God was going to do what He said He would do _____

H.

1. Since Jesus healed those who came and asked Him, it's nearly impossible for me to doubt that anyone who asks for healing will be healed _____

2. When I pray for healing I know it's done _____

3. God has used me in many occasions as a conduit to manifest healing in many people _____

4. I hate sickness and diseases with all my heart, we were not created to be sick. This is why when I see someone who is sick, I always have to pray for them _____

5. After I have intimacy with God there is a strong desire in me to see all people be healed from all their afflictions_____

I.

1. I often have visions or dreams of me raising someone from the dead or praying for someone's limb to grow back ____

2. On countless occasions, I've felt God's power rest on me to pray for someone who could not see or could not walk or could not talk _____

3. When I see someone who is crippled I always hate that they have to suffer and I'm always moved by compassion to pray for them ____

4. I always have a strong desire to be used by God to showcase His power to the world _____

5. If someone cannot see, hear, speak because of an ailment I'm often moved by God to fast and pray for their breakthrough _____

A. Various kinds of Tongues _____

B. Interpretation of Tongues _____

C. Prophecy _____

D. Word of Knowledge _____

E. Word of Wisdom _____

F. Discernment of Spirits _____

G. Faith _____

H. Healing _____

I. The Working of Miracles _____

The Parenting Gifts: My Body

1 Never me **2** Almost never me **3** Sometimes me **4** Almost always me **5** Always me

A.

1. I have a passion to start new projects _____

2. I don't mind where I live as long as it's where God wants me to be, so moving from place to place although difficult at times is ok with me _____

3. I'm zealous about the foundational truths of the Bible; if your foundation is not steady, your life will not be either _____

4. I teach but I'm not a teacher, I preach but I'm not a preacher, I evangelize but I'm not an evangelist, I prophecy but I'm not a prophet _____

5. I feel called to plant churches every and anywhere, share the gospel to every tongue, and do or oversee the discipleship process_____

B.

1. I see or hear things from the spirit world and sometimes I know I have to tell someone what I saw; this feeling never leaves me until I obey _____

2. God gives me revelations about his heart for people on a regular basis _____

3. Repentance is of the utmost importance to me, without Holiness we cannot see God _____

4. I get dreams and visions for people and for the church Continuously

_____

5. When I go somewhere God shows me or tells me what's going to happen

before it happens _____

C.

1. I feel compelled to share Christ all the time and everywhere I go _____

2. I do not like staying in a church building. When I'm outside sharing Christ, I

feel alive _____

3. I think of creative ways of how we could win souls for the Kingdom of God

and I also implement these ideas _____

4. My heart is continuously burning for the lost _____

5. The most important message is the Cross of Jesus Christ, and every time I

preach or speak I always have to share the message of the cross because

we are lost without him _____

D.

1. It is my duty to protect the people of God even from themselves _____

2. I don't feel I have to go everywhere and preach, I know I have to go

somewhere and preach _____

3. I'm comfortable laying roots somewhere _____

4. When God gives me a vision for a place he also will use me to accomplish

it _____

5. I feel called to walk with people from the start of their relationship with God to the end of it _____

E.

1. I enjoy explaining concepts more than I do just informing people about things _____

2. It's hard for me to leave a place after sharing unless I know that they understood what I said _____

3. I enjoy putting together curriculum and coaching people through them _____

4. I'd rather stay somewhere and instruct people than go from place to place and preach _____

5. I love being informed, people die for the lack of knowledge so we must study to show ourselves approved, I believe this and I live it out _____

A. Apostle _____

B. Prophet _____

C. Evangelist _____

D. Pastor _____

E. Teacher _____

Notes

Chapter 4

1. *"Definition Of ZEAL". 2019. Merriam-Webster.Com. https://www.merriam-webster.com/dictionary/zeal.*

Chapter 9

1. *Health, Fresh. 2019. "A Safe Place For Pastors And Their Spouses Who Are Experiencing Weariness, Burnout And/Or Crisis In Ministry - Fresh Hope For Mental Health". Fresh Hope For Mental Health. http://freshhopeformentalhealth.com/a-safe-place-for-pastors-and-their-spouses-who-are-experiencing-weariness-burnout-andor-crisis-in-ministry/.*

2. *Anon, (2019). [online] Available at: https://www.blueletterbible.org/lang/lexicon/lexicon.cfm?t=kjv&strongs=g1249 [Accessed 30 Aug. 2019].*

Chapter 10

1. *"Genesis 1:1 (ESV)". 2019. Blue Letter Bible.*

    https://www.blueletterbible.org/lang/lexicon/lexicon.cfm?t=ESV&strongs=h1984.

Chapter 11

1. *2019. Worldpopulationreview.Com. http://worldpopulationreview.com/us-cities/cut-bank-mt-population/.*

2. *Research, LifeWay, Church Toolkit, Custom Research, – Categories, American Views, Church Life, and Discipleship Canada et al. 2019. "Lifeway Research: Americans Are Fond Of The Bible, Don'T Actually Read It". Lifeway Research.*

    https://lifewayresearch.com/2017/04/25/lifeway-research-americans-are-fond-of-the-bible-dont-actually-read-it/.

3. *"John 11:35 (ESV)". 2019. Blue Letter Bible.*

    https://www.blueletterbible.org/lang/lexicon/lexicon.cfm?Strongs=G1145&t=ESV.

4. *Edmondson, Ron, Craig Blomberg, The Blog, Inside BST, Craig Blomberg, and Stephen*

    Altrogge. 2019. "John 11 Commentary - Matthew Henry Commentary On The Whole

    Bible (Concise)". Bible Study Tools.

    https://www.biblestudytools.com/commentaries/matthew-henry-concise/john/11.html.

Chapter 12

1. *2019. Myersbriggs.Org. https://www.myersbriggs.org/my-mbti-personality-type/mbti-*

    basics/thinking-or-feeling.htm?bhcp=1.

2. *"Definition Of MORES". 2019. Merriam-Webster.Com. https://www.merriam-*

    webster.com/dictionary/mores.

Chapter 13

1. *"John Gills Exposition Of The Bible Commentary". 2019. Bible Study Tools.*

    https://www.biblestudytools.com/commentaries/gills-exposition-of-the-bible/.

2. *Deffinbaug, Robert L. 2019. "30. Thinking Straight About Spiritual Gifts (Romans 12:3-8)*

    | Bible.Org". Bible.Org. https://bible.org/seriespage/30-thinking-straight-about-spiritual-

    gifts-romans-123-8.

3. *"Why Did Martin Luther Reject James?". 2019. Biblestudy.Org.*

    http://www.biblestudy.org/question/why-did-martin-luther-want-book-of-james-out-of-

    bible.html.

Chapter 14

1. *"Strong's Greek: 1248. Διακονία (Diakonia) -- Service, Ministry". 2019. Biblehub.Com.*

    http://biblehub.com/greek/1248.htm.

2. *"The Amazing Name Martha: Meaning And Etymology". 2019. Abarim Publications.*

    http://www.abarim-publications.com/Meaning/Martha.html#.XSSp9yVMEIQ.

Chapter 15

1. *"Strong's Greek: 1321. Διδάσκω (Didaskó) -- To Teach". 2019. Biblehub.Com. http://biblehub.com/greek/1321.htm.*

Chapter 16

1. *"Strong's Greek: 3870. Παρακαλέω (Parakaleó) -- To Call To Or For, To Exhort, To Encourage". 2019. Biblehub.Com. http://biblehub.com/greek/3870.htm.*

2. *"Definition Of Admonish | Dictionary.Com". 2019. Www.Dictionary.Com. http://www.dictionary.com/browse/admonish.*

Chapter 17

1. *"Strong's Greek: 2130. Εὐμετάδοτος (Eumetadotos) -- Ready To Impart". 2019. Biblehub.Com. http://biblehub.com/greek/2130.htm.*

2. *"Acts 10:10 Commentaries: But He Became Hungry And Was Desiring To Eat; But While They Were Making Preparations, He Fell Into A Trance;". 2019. Biblehub.Com. https://biblehub.com/commentaries/acts/10-10.htm.*

Chapter 21

1. *C. K. Barrett, A Commentary on the First Epistle to the Corinthians (Hagerstown, NY: Harper & Row, 1817), 1.*
2. *C.K. Barret*
3. *F. F. Bruce, New Century Bible 1 and 2 Corrinthians (London, England: The Attic Press, 1917), 2.*
4. *Leon Morris, 1 Corinthians (Grand Rapids, Michigan: William B. Eerdmans 1985), 18.*

Chapter 28

1. *Edmondson, Ron, Craig Blomberg, The Blog, Inside BST, Craig Blomberg, and Stephen Altrogge. 2019. "Topos - New Testament Greek Lexicon - New American Standard". Bible Study Tools. https://www.biblestudytools.com/lexicons/greek/nas/topos.html.*

Chapter 29

1. "How Often Do We Dream | Sleep.Org". 2019. Sleep.Org.
   https://www.sleep.org/articles/how-often-dreams/.

Chapter 30

1. "Notitia Definition And Meaning | Collins English Dictionary". 2019.
   Collinsdictionary.Com. https://www.collinsdictionary.com/us/dictionary/english/notitia.

2. Mahoney, Kevin. 2019. "Latin Definition For: Assensus, Assensus (ID: 5099) - Latin
   Dictionary And Grammar Resources - Latdict". Latin-Dictionary.Net. http://latin-
   dictionary.net/definition/5099/assensus-assensus.

Chapter 32

1. Kittel, Gerhard. 1964. Theological Dictionary Of The New Testatment Vol 1. Grand
   Rapids Michigan: Wm Eerdmans.

Chapter 33

1. "Interlinear Bible: Greek, Hebrew, Transliterated, English, Strong's". 2019.
   Biblehub.Com. https://biblehub.com/interlinear/.

2. "Strong's Greek: 1755. Ἐνέργημα (Energéma) -- An Effect, Operation". 2019.
   Biblehub.Com. https://biblehub.com/greek/1755.htm.

3. "Strong's Greek: 1411. Δύναμις (Dunamis) -- (Miraculous) Power, Might, Strength".
   2019. Biblehub.Com. https://biblehub.com/greek/1411.htm.

4. 2019. Crashstats.Nhtsa.Dot.Gov.
   https://crashstats.nhtsa.dot.gov/Api/Public/ViewPublication/809911.

Chapter 34

1. Us, Contact, and Guest Post?. 2019. "Stats". Fatherhood Factor.
   https://fatherhoodfactor.com/us-fatherless-statistics/.

2. Fatherhood Factor

Chapter 37

1. *Edmondson, Ron, Craig Blomberg, The Blog, Inside BST, Craig Blomberg, and Stephen Altrogge. 2019. "Naioth Definition And Meaning - Bible Dictionary". Bible Study Tools. https://www.biblestudytools.com/dictionary/naioth/.*

Chapter 39

1. *MacArthur, John. 1986. Ephesians Macarthur New Testament Commentary. Chicago: Moody Publishers.*

2. *Green, Joel B. n.d. Dictionary Of Jesus And The Gospels.*

3. *"Definition Of Domineering | Dictionary.Com". 2019. Www.Dictionary.Com. https://www.dictionary.com/browse/domineering.*

Chapter 40

1. *"Strong's Greek: 5198. Ὑγιαίνω (Hugiainó) -- To Be Sound, Healthy". 2019. Biblehub.Com. https://biblehub.com/greek/5198.htm.*

Made in the USA
Lexington, KY
09 November 2019